Edited by Ivor Indyk

SHELTERED

The Giramondo Publishing Company
for the Writing and Society Research Group
University of Western Sydney

First published 2006 by the
Giramondo Publishing Company
PO Box 752 Artarmon NSW 1570

www.giramondopublishing.com

Designed by
Harry Williamson
Formatted and typeset in
11/14 Garamond 3 by
Andrew Davies
Printed and bound by
Southwood Press
Distributed in Australia by
Tower Books

Sheltered Lives
(HEAT 11, New series, 2006)
ISBN 1 920882 16 2
ISSN 1326-1460

Cover: Noel McKenna
Yellow House, Merrylands, (2005)
oil on canvas, 60 x 70cm
See pp.97–112

The editor acknowledges the
support given by the following
organisations:

The University of Western Sydney

The Australian Government
through the Australia Council,
its arts funding and advisory body

The NSW Government –
Ministry of the Arts

Arts Victoria

Sydney Grammar School

Acknowledgements

SYDNEY GRAMMAR SCHOOL

ASSISTANT EDITORS:
CHRISTOPHER CYRILL (FICTION), LUCY
DOUGAN (POETRY), SARAH KANOWSKI
(NON-FICTION), ADAM AITKEN (SPECIAL
PROJECTS), ANTONI JACH (MELBOURNE
EDITOR), RICHARD LEVER (COPY EDITOR),
KATHLEEN OLIVE (ADMINISTRATION)

EDITORIAL ADVISORY BOARD:
ADRIAN MARTIN, ANNA COUANI,
MARTIN DUWELL, KEVIN HART,
NICHOLAS JOSE, EVELYN JUERS,
VRASIDAS KARALIS, CASSANDRA PYBUS,
IMRE SALUSINSZKY, JOHN SUTHERLAND

Correspondence and contributions:
HEAT
Dean's Unit, Arts (Bankstown)
University of Western Sydney
Locked Bag 1797 Penrith South DC
NSW 1797 Australia
Tel: (02) 9772 6350
heat@uws.edu.au

All published contributions by
academics are refereed.

Subscriptions:
Giramondo Publishing Company
PO Box 752 Artarmon NSW 1570
Tel: (61 2) 9772 6350
Fax: (61 2) 9419 7934
heat@giramondopublishing.com
www.giramondopublishing.com/heat

Annual rates (two issues)
$44 in Australia and New Zealand
$55 international
Institutional subscriptions
$68 in Australia and New Zealand
$78 international
Amounts are in Australian dollars
Australian rates include GST

Contents

This issue is dedicated to
Jenya Osborne
13 October 1940 – 10 March 2006

Tom Cho

Two Stories

Tom Cho is writing a collection of short fiction that explores the themes of identity and popular culture. He is completing a PhD in Professional Writing at Deakin University and works at Footscray Community Arts Centre. Visit him at http://www.diadic.com/Tom/

The Sound of Music

At first, all you can see are clouds, then an aerial view of mountains, then a green valley, and a lake, and suddenly an open grassy area, and then there's me, spinning around with my arms outstretched and I'm singing. It's interesting, really, because I remember how my Auntie Ling used to do exactly the same thing. Like me, Auntie Ling loved music, and she loved being out in the hills, singing. In China, Auntie Ling was a river-boat gambler who loved to sing but could not find any singing work. She migrated to Australia in search of a better life, and now she is an officer in the Danish Imperial Navy who lives in a beautiful mansion in France. At any rate, I soon realise that I do not have time to think about Auntie Ling. This is because the bells of the abbey have started ringing. I am going to be late for chapel so I run to the abbey. Unfortunately, I return to the abbey to find that Mother Superior has made arrangements for me to look after the children of a Captain von Trapp.

So, a few days later, I pack my bags and go to Captain von Trapp's house. It turns out that Captain von Trapp is very cold to me, and I find myself being worried about whether he likes me or not. Yet, through a process of winning the hearts of the von Trapp children and disobeying the Captain's orders and talking with the Captain about 80s television shows and pop songs, Captain von Trapp and I eventually end up becoming much closer. In fact, it is not long before Captain von Trapp and I are having sex and falling in love.

Once we have gotten together, I find myself incredibly drawn to Captain von Trapp, and he to me. We start spending a great deal of time with each other; we want to be together all the time. As a result, by the end of the month, we are already finishing each other's sentences and laughing at exactly the same time and in exactly the same way. We start dressing alike. We start walking alike. We even start having the same desires and ambitions. At times, I find myself wondering if so much commonality between two people is a good thing. How do you solve a problem like co-dependency?

But, the thing is, it eventually becomes apparent that Captain von Trapp and I are not merging in a typical 'couples' sense. In fact, it soon becomes obvious that something quite different is happening. What is happening is this: I am starting to become more and more like Captain von Trapp. I have begun wearing clothes that are very similar to the Captain's clothes. I have begun to copy the Captain's gestures. I have begun to insist that people call me 'Captain'. There is so much about the Captain that I like. There is the air of confidence that surrounds him. There is his ability to look so good in a suit. There is the way that his stern manner commands authority. He is wealthy and sophisticated. He is even a good dancer. No wonder I find it incredibly satisfying to emulate a man like him.

However, this state of affairs soon raises various issues. In particular, the question 'How do you solve a problem like co-dependency?' is soon replaced by a more pressing question: Can who you like to 'do' also be bound up in issues of who you are or want to be? Unfortunately, Captain von Trapp is in no mood to explore this question. He becomes uneasy about these changes in me and we start to argue about the new me. He tries to take a disciplinary approach with me. He orders me to stop answering the telephone as him. He becomes angry when other people mistake me for him. He tries to stop me repeating everything he says a second after he says it. I do not blame him for his anger and discomfort but it eventually forces me to flee back to the abbey.

Within the walls of the abbey, I seek the counsel of Mother Superior. I ask her: Can who you like to 'do' also be bound up in issues of who you are or want to be? Interestingly, when I pose this question to her, she abruptly confesses to me that she has always wanted to have sex with The Fonz from *Happy Days*. As soon as she says this, she looks away from me. But I immediately tell her that I am a huge fan of The Fonz and that I grew up being inspired by The Fonz as a role model of masculinity. When Mother Superior hears this, she looks a little more at ease. I then confess to her my own secret Fonz-related fantasy: I am The Fonz, looking really cool and handsome, and I am standing in the centre of a room wearing a leather jacket and jeans. I click my fingers. Suddenly, some other really cool and handsome guys wearing leather jackets and jeans run up to me and drape themselves seductively over me and begin stroking my hair. These really cool and handsome guys then click their fingers. Suddenly, more really cool and handsome guys wearing leather jackets and jeans run up and drape themselves seductively over the first set of really cool and handsome guys and begin stroking their hair. This second set of really cool and handsome guys then click their fingers. Suddenly, even more really cool and handsome guys wearing leather jackets and jeans run up and drape themselves seductively over this second set of really cool and handsome guys and begin stroking their hair. This pattern continues until the room is completely filled with really cool and handsome guys wearing leather jackets and jeans who are draped seductively over each other and are stroking each other's hair and I as The Fonz am in the centre of it all. Once she hears the relatively more excessive nature of my Fonz-related fantasy, Mother Superior looks relieved. We look at each other and we smile.

Mother Superior then takes my hand and tells me that, if I am impressionable enough to want to model myself upon someone else, then I should have the courage to live out my fantasy. She urges me to escape from Austria and to go and find peace in Switzerland living as someone like Captain von Trapp. I try to tell Mother Superior that it is simplistic just to say that I am impressionable: in a sense, aren't we all composites of the influences of various entities in our lives – family members, friends, lovers, certain people we watch on TV, characters we read in books, etc, etc? And surely some of these things are influential because they do appeal to our fantasies? And yet, while our fantasies allow us the pleasure of imagining who we might be, can't they also make us painfully conscious of who we currently are? But Mother Superior is too busy singing the song 'Climb Ev'ry Mountain' to listen to me properly. At any rate, Mother Superior is right about me going to Switzerland to live as someone like Captain von Trapp. So I go and pack for my trip, choosing the kinds of clothes that the Captain would wear. The Nazis have closed the borders so I must journey to Switzerland on foot. But, eventually, I make it to the Austrian mountains and this is where I am to be seen, climbing the mountains to a different kind of life in Switzerland. There I am, walking up a mountain, looking and acting like Captain von Trapp as a chorus sings 'Climb Ev'ry Mountain', and then there is a wider shot of the surrounding countryside with its lakes and greenery, and then an aerial shot of the mountains, and, finally, all you can see are clouds.

Today on Dr Phil

Today my Auntie Lien and I are appearing on the television show of the famed psychologist Dr Phil. The *Dr Phil* episode we are appearing in is titled 'What are you really mad at?' and Dr Phil is asking Auntie Lien and me about how we deal with anger. Auntie Lien is right in the middle of talking about her propensity to explode in anger when Dr Phil asks her why she gets angry so easily. Auntie Lien hesitates. Dr Phil advises her, 'You've got to face it to replace it.' Hearing Dr Phil say this prompts Auntie Lien to confess that her anger stems from the many difficulties she has experienced with relationships. She says that she has been unlucky in love. Furthermore, she says that the sadder she gets, the angrier she gets. I feel that I can relate to this statement and so I join the studio audience in enthusiastically applauding my auntie's comment. Auntie Lien suddenly says something in Ancient Greek. Dr Phil looks at her blankly, and she explains that she was quoting from *Medea*, the classic play by Euripides. She confesses that she likes to study the work of the great Athenian dramatists. She translates the lines for Dr Phil: 'The fiercest anger of all, the most incurable/ Is that which rages in the place of dearest love.' As Auntie Lien goes on to discuss in minute detail the structural imperfections in Euripidean drama that have puzzled scholars for centuries, I can tell that Dr Phil and the studio audience are struck by the fact that they are sharing a room with one of the finest scholars of Ancient Greek drama that the world has seen. Me, I have always found it interesting that Auntie Lien has such a great mind for scholarly pursuits as well as such a great capacity for flying into fits of anger. This makes me think about my own experiences with intellectualism and anger. Sometimes I have a tendency to 'intellectualise first and get angry later'. Interestingly, like many people, when I get really angry I can transform into what seems like a completely different person. This makes me turn to Dr Phil to ask him: If anger can transform me, in what other ways might anger be transformative? I suggest to him that perhaps I could use my anger creatively, even proactively. For example, surely some of the most significant political revolutions in history have been in part driven by a sense of rage? This then leads me consider my attraction to anger. Could it be that I associate anger with power? This would be ironic, given that anger can occur as a consequence of not feeling powerful enough. But Dr Phil is too absorbed in Auntie Lien's discussion of the function of the chorus in Ancient Greek drama to listen to me properly. However, eventually the topic turns back to anger when Dr Phil begins reflecting upon the murderous actions of the character of Medea following her betrayal by her husband. In fact, Dr Phil declares that Medea ably demonstrates his belief that people who experience un-controllable rage actually have unfulfilled needs that must be addressed. Hearing this makes me think of my own life, and so I confess to Dr Phil a fantasy that I have recently had. In this fantasy, I become extremely angry. The fantasy begins with me starting to sweat from my anger. My heart starts beating faster. I clench my fists and the anger makes my face heat up. In this fantasy, I am like The Incredible Hulk in that the angrier I get, the stronger I get. So my muscles start to grow. My muscles become so big that they start to outgrow my clothes. The seams of my shirt and pants begin to split. My neck becomes thicker, and my thighs and calves swell and become harder. I am growing and growing, putting on height as well as bulk, and soon I am around eight feet tall and full of strength and fury. First I go rampaging through the streets, smashing things out of sheer anger. No one is stronger than me. I can bend lampposts and break walls and throw cars. It does not take long for the police and the military to be sent after me. But they cannot stop me. Their guns and explosives only make me angrier and stronger. I rip apart their trucks and tanks. Then I move on to the sheer satisfaction of destroying whole buildings. After a good hour of smashing and destroying, I stomp all the way to my girlfriend's house. She opens the door and looks a little surprised to see me. I am standing before her, breathing hard and still very angry. She says to me, 'I was just watching you on the news. You were destroying all these buildings. You should have more respect for the property of others.' I pause for a moment before replying, 'Don't make me angry. You wouldn't like me when I'm angry.' I enjoy saying this line to her – it is what Dr Banner used to say before he turned into

The Hulk. But, as it turns out, my girlfriend does like me when I'm angry. She begins looking at my muscles in admiration. I glare at her but that only makes her sigh happily. This just makes me glare at her all the more. I am so angry. The angrier I get, the stronger I get. And the stronger I get, the more aroused she gets. She looks at me and her face begins to flush. Her breath starts to quicken. And the more aroused she gets, the younger she gets. She used to be thirty-three but now she is getting younger. She smiles and winks at me as she goes back into her twenties. Fascinated, I watch as she gets younger and younger, and she doesn't stop until she is in her teens and blushing and cuter than ever. And the younger she gets, the fewer people she has had sex with. She slips her hand into mine and tells me that she is sixteen years old and a virgin and that she is eager for me to teach her all about sex. So I scoop her up in my arms and take her to her bedroom and we spend all night having the hottest sex you can imagine. After I have finished telling Dr Phil my anger fantasy, there is complete silence in the studio. I had been hoping that the audience would enthusiastically applaud my fantasy but they just stare at me. It is then that I wonder if I have said too much. Finally, Dr Phil breaks the silence to tell me, 'You have to name it before you can claim it,' and he encourages me to look inside myself to work out what I really want in life. He then says that we have run out of time and so he faces the camera to deliver a final address about the issues we have spoken about today. He begins to deliver a very moving address about how life is managed, not cured. As Dr Phil speaks, I think about the pain that anger can cause and I start to feel sad. I look at Auntie Lien's face and I can tell that she is feeling sad about this too. In fact, the more poignantly Dr Phil speaks, the sadder Auntie Lien gets. But then I remember that the sadder Auntie Lien gets, the angrier she gets. I soon notice that she is clenching and unclenching her fists. Her eyes dart around the room in agitation. As Dr Phil continues to speak, she begins to mutter angrily under her breath. Finally, it is too much for her. She explodes in anger, jumping out of her seat and attacking Dr Phil. Security guards run up to the stage and try to pull Dr Phil and Auntie Lien apart. The studio audience is hollering and chanting and Auntie Lien is swearing so colourfully that her words will have to be bleeped out before the episode goes to air. Auntie Lien calls out to encourage me to join in the fisticuffs. I am unsure about this but she reminds me that releasing anger can be very satisfying. The thing is, Auntie Lien has a point — quite a valid point that not even Dr Phil has raised. But first, I take the time to intellectualise about Dollard et al.'s Frustration-Aggression Hypothesis and its subsequent behaviourist/neo-associationist reformulation by Berkowitz. Having considered this and its implications for research on factors affecting aggression, I become angry and join Auntie Lien in releasing my rage. As Auntie Lien and I engage in a dramatic punch-up with Dr Phil and his security guards, the show's end credits start to roll. A few people in the studio audience begin to applaud. Auntie Lien and I still have plenty of rage left but, soon, the show will be over.

Anna Poletti, editor

A People's History of Australian Zines

Anna Poletti
Kane Barwick
Lachlan Musicman
Lou
Amber Carvan
Vanessa Berry

Anna Poletti

Introduction

'The desire begins with the demand to live not as an object but as a subject
of history – to live as if something actually depended on one's actions – and
that demand opens onto a free street.'
Greil Marcus, *Lipstick Traces: A Secret History of the Twentieth Century*

Despite the reactions of those encountering zines for the first time,
zines are not a new formation on the Australian cultural landscape. At
least, not for those who have grown up with them, or passed through
the decades-old zine culture on their way to other destinations. Yet
the stubborn covertness of zine culture, its refusal to stand for long in
the light of mainstream attention, gives most people's first contact
with the publications and their associated communities the feel of
invention, of zines having only existed for the time it took that first
zine they've found to be produced. Indeed it is this feeling of discovering a hitherto invisible cultural world, which unfolds before you the
more you traverse its territory, that is part of the unending charm of
zines. To some extent this veneer of newness is due to the ceaseless
flow of zine-makers through the zine culture; some appear for barely
a season, spending a summer feverishly putting out several issues and
capturing attention, only to disappear as the days shorten. Other
zine-makers such as Vanessa Berry, who contributes a piece to this
collection, have been self-publishers for a decade or more, and while
their output is sporadic, their presence reminds us that zines are a
fixed presence in some lives.

Zines are independently produced publications which range in
length from one to fifty pages. Predominantly photocopied and hand-
bound, they often include handcrafted features, original covers, stamps,
post-it-notes, photographs and collage. They may have several editors
and contributing writers, or they may be the work of a single producer
(known as a 'zinester'). Zines can contain writing, comics, drawings,
photographs, stolen text and stencils; and the topics are limited only
by the imagination of the person producing the zine. Some are dedicated to a specific, often odd theme, such as the zine *Toast,* which offers

recipes for meals involving toast, while others cover broader topics, such as *Foffle*, a zine which celebrates the outer-limits of kitsch in Australian popular culture. Zines speak to and seek out communities of people united by their interests, obsessions and ultimately a love of homemade communication.

As a genre, zines have their roots in the British punk movement of the 1970s and, some argue, the political pamphleteering of the American Revolution; independent, unmediated communication is the common ground between punks and the political agitators of fledgling America. Zines also share in the history of mail-art, visual artists' explorations of reproduction and photocopy, and campus newspapers. In the contemporary context, it is the practice of handmade communication in an increasingly digitised society which creates a zine community.

I began reading zines in 1999 after attending the National Young Writers Festival in Newcastle. An event conceived in the aftermath of Mark Davis' *Gangland: Cultural Elites and the New Generationalism*, the festival was designed as a platform for young writers working in traditional and subcultural mediums. The first Australian literary event to include the zine in its programming, the 1999 festival offered sessions dedicated to zine production and distribution, and attracted zine-makers from several states. In 2002, while undertaking doctoral research on Australian zines as an autobiographical form at the University of Newcastle, I started my own zine, titled *Trade Entrance* – perhaps the epitome of niche publishing. Aimed primarily at the zine-makers whose work I was studying, *Trade Entrance* sought to 'demystify' the academic process for the zinesters who were its subject, while also acting as a journal which recorded the development of my research. I hoped that my zine would contribute to the zine community while my academic work reflected upon it.

As the essays in this collection illustrate, while zine-makers come and go, zines are always in circulation; on the floors of independent book and record stores, in on-line distribution catalogues, given away at gigs or exhibition openings, lent and borrowed between friends, arriving in mailboxes all over the country. It is this continued presence, the ensconced status of zines in the backstreets of Australia's cultural life, which has inspired this 'People's History of Australian Zines'. Rather than offer up a more traditional explanatory article of what zine culture is, how it operates and what defines a zine, I decided upon a collection of short, personal pieces from past and present zine-makers as a more fitting way to introduce people to the zine phenomenon. The collection also aims to give those who have participated in Australia's zine culture pause for reflection, and perhaps a new perspective on those raggy little booklets which they may've come to take for granted.

It is tenable, but perhaps quite parochial, to speak of generations of zine-makers in Australia. Murdoch University Library in Perth holds a collection of Australian science fiction fanzines which stretches back to the 1950s, and includes such titles as *Antipodes*, which was published in Carlton, the periodical *The Australian Science Fiction Newsletter*, and issues one, three and four of *?*, published by Amateur Fantasy Publications Australia in 1953–54. These early fanzines presented original fiction, reviews and articles on science fiction, and connected readers and writers across Australia through mailing lists. The National Library of Australia also holds zines, including several examples of women's publications such as *Girl's own* fanzine produced in 1973, *Purrzine* published in the 1990s, and *Gynaezine* published in 2003. Through the independent music zines of the 1980s and 90s, to the short fiction publications of the 1990s, and the autobiographical zines of the present century, there are many contemporary authors, journalists, designers, comic artists and publishers who have zine experience.

Nevertheless, zine culture is a tributary of Australian culture which has been particularly resistant to summarisation or clear definition. Partly because of the ceaseless change in its membership, Australia's zine-makers do not take up an artistic or literary tradition and strive for its continued refinement. Perhaps zines retain the feeling of a 'new medium' because as each new reader is transformed into a zine-maker, it is as though the zine-form starts again. As the new writer-cum-publisher learns the ropes, and distributes his or her victories and mistakes amongst a diverse readership, the zine-form is re-invented.

The essays in this collection give us some indication of what individual zine-makers have gained from their engagements with the process of self-publishing. For Kane Barwick, zines were a place to begin writing, where a relationship with style, content, and deadlines was first developed. Lachlan Musicman presents zines as a place where politics and opinions can be tested, where one's identity as a 'political animal' can find expression. For several of the contributors, zines and the communities formed around them were ways of exploring the possibilities and limitations of community. For others not represented in this collection, such as the perennial self-publisher ΠO, the zine community is one space among many where new literary works can find an audience.

Moreover, it is as an audience that the zine community really comes into its own. At a time when the 'above-ground' literary community laments the decline of Australian publishing and the limited number of readers willing to take a risk in their choices, zine readers are compelling in their willingness to adventure far-and-wide in their reading habits. An example of this can be found in Sticky, Australia's only zine store, located in a subway corridor in Melbourne, where an anonymous novella which is photocopied and bound with twine and duct tape, has developed a following. *It'll be morning* sells to gaggles of high school students, commuters and others who wander through the door, many of whom are visitors to Melbourne from interstate or overseas. With its sparse, rough presentation, the book feels dangerous, somewhat illicit, an impression increased by the enigmatic absence of an author's name, replaced by an email address on the inside back cover. *It'll be morning* is a great example of how the contemporary self-published text, selling for five dollars, can capture an audience without the seemingly ubiquitous elaborate cover design of contemporary fiction, or the force of an author's reputation behind it. The articles in this collection testify not only to the pleasures of zine-making, but also to that feeling of opening onto a 'free street', which is a vital and

invigorating element of the zine-reading experience.

The 'free street' is an image conjured by Greil Marcus in his attempt to capture the possibilities and demands of the British punk movement of the 1970s. As descendents of that movement, which had a strong fanzine component, contemporary Australian zinesters have inherited the hurried urgency of the punk 'do-it-yourself' aesthetic. The ideals of open access to the tools of cultural production defined the vibrancy and immediacy of punk, and a sense of urgency remains an essential part of many people's involvement with contemporary zines. Lachlan Musicman describes this urgency in his love for 'half-arsed' zines, a colloquial term for an undertaking performed in a hurry or left incomplete. It is not just a lack of will or workmanship that is responsible for the 'half-arsed' production values of many zines. Like letters and diaries, zines are often written with a compulsion, which most zine-makers describe in terms of 'a need' to record and reflect. For many, zine-making is fuelled by an impulse to document and to discuss objects and events which may not appear to have any significance, those things which slip through the formalised structures charged with the documenting of history. In recent Australian zines one can find a history of the Pelaco Shirt brand (*Secondhand Rose*), reflections on the demolishing of Melbourne's iconically bland Gas and Fuel Buildings to make way for Federation Square (*I think So...*), and 'a history of astronaut fashion' (*Nerdling*). On the surface these articles are entertaining diversions, but they belie a preoccupation amongst those writing zines 'to live not as an object but as a subject of history', to adopt an active role in the culture by documenting and celebrating its minutiae. In this light, much of the non-fiction writing in zines can be viewed both as amateur history-writing and as cultural analysis concerned with the quotidian, a form of people's history-writing which may prove to be valuable as documents of the everyday, just as the punk fanzines of the 1970s such as *Sniffin Glue* have become essential documents in the cultural history of punk.

The publication *Milkbar*, remembered by Amber Carvan in her essay 'Monopoly Millionaires', is a particularly strong example of a self-published enterprise born from the commitment to documentation and critical reflection. *Milkbar*'s topic of analysis, Australian zine culture itself, proved to be a provocative one, causing much debate and discussion within the zine community about the possibilities of a critical element in zine culture. Carvan's and Barwick's contributions give us some insight into how the competing values and aims at work within the zine network have influenced individual self-publishers to strive for excellence, while others remain proudly 'half-arsed'. While the founders of *Milkbar* sought to foster a culture of rigorous debate and the evaluation of zines and their potential, Lou on the other hand offers a perspective on zines which exalts them as ephemeral, transitory objects of exchange which 'are almost too slight to hold the meaning they're given'.

Anna Poletti recently completed a PhD at The University of Newcastle investigating Australian zines as a contemporary autobiographical form. She makes the zine *Trade Entrance* and volunteers at Melbourne's zine store Sticky.

Kane Barwick
It was here for a while

I've told the story quite a number of times so I'm certainly in no hurry to tell it again, let's just agree: It began. At first I proudly called it *Surezine* (one word) but later simply *Sure*.

It lasted nineteen issues; though it isn't yet officially dead the name seems to have gone into 'retirement' as a friend once remarked. Twenty issues was my lofty goal. By issue nineteen I hadn't the energy for photocopying or envelope stuffing. I sent an email-only affair to twenty people, though I suspect only half of them read it. My mum said that last issue was far too morose. I thought it contained some of the best writing of my life, but there you go.

For the entire seven years it existed I was often proud of and always very attached to *Sure*. It received attention and made me friends, not the sort of friends who get one places but the sort of friends one trusts above all others. After all those years and all that effort the end result was boxes of unsold zines, and self-confidence in myself as a writer. In its own way *Sure* rewrote my future. That's not exactly true. *Sure* wrote my future. When I started publishing, I was twenty-one, annoyed, frightened and resolutely lost.

Today, I am twenty-nine, a little lost, mildly frightened but almost certainly a writer who believes he can and should write.

I kept *Sure* afloat because I admired it, because there were other ideas I wanted to explore, other fonts I wanted to use, other art to be butchered and displayed on the cover and because I wasn't sure where else to go. I mean, after all that time being in absolute control, what could possibly follow? A great number of people who once published zines no longer do anything at all creative. Gone. Though a number write professionally or turn out art in other mediums, people like me are afraid to sever their links with the 'general public.' (I use inverted commas because the number of people who paid for and read an edition of *Sure* hardly constituted the public at large. Though I couldn't say exactly who the one to two hundred regular *Sure* readers were, I would suggest that a vast number were also zine creators whom I'd met or people who knew someone who knew me and, in their own way, were supporting me as you would a friend who cooked an awful chocolate cake but said, 'My what a lovely cake'. Having to go out and face the real (read: none-zine) world filled me with terror, out there a real publisher could really tell me what's wrong with my writing. You see, and this relates to 'zine' being removed from *Surezine*, the zine world is inconceivably small; where one zine-maker protects the other, where feathers are easily ruffled when someone decides to break out of the mould and do something a little contrary. To most people, this is the inverse of the perception of zines as a free and highly improvised world. While on the surface challenging 'norms' (which norms I couldn't honestly say) was the meat and potatoes of such a medium, what was most ardently adhered to was togetherness. And by togetherness I mean not rocking the boat. And by that I mean, you'll get jumped on when you step out of line. And by that I mean, if you even dare criticise another zine, you make yourself canon fodder in a very insular world.

Here's the shorthand: a zine is its creator; when you criticise the zine you criticise the person; the person who poured his or her heart and soul into the zine (me, I poured money and fear of failure into *Sure*) has given everything to belong, and should be welcomed with open arms (the rule is, all zine-makers are 'outsiders' and hence deserve to be 'inside' at least one clique); the zine-maker should most certainly not be criticised like a painter, an author, an actor, a director, (i.e. a real artist) because the zine world is not the real world.

More short hand: I removed the word 'zine' from *Sure* because I became too embarrassed to be associated with such an innocuous yet hostile world. I continued to publish *Sure* for three or four more years.

This was good. Very good in fact. There came a point whenI was certain who my friends were and were not. From that point on – the point when I truly believed that I hadn't any interest in what any one person thought of me or *Sure* – it was something I could be proud of. I stopped pretending to care about 'issues' of any kind, rather I wrote and wrote and wrote. My friends, whose development had in some ways mirrored my own, also grew more confident in their writing. Together we were beginning to believe in our talents. From interviews and first-hand diatribes grew more and more sophisticated fiction. From a magazine jammed to the hilt with twenty to fifty separate pieces I began publishing *Sure* with only one, two or three long pieces. Pure fiction. Often regrettable and not very sophisticated at all, but absolutely unhindered by the influence of the 'community' of zine-makers.

Sure became most important to me when I felt completely free. *Sure* at its best was not a zine, it was nothing in particular. It was a way for me to test myself: if I created an issue deadline I had no choice but to write. And yeah, conceited or not, I had the gall to charge people money for what I'd written.

This to me is the essence of a zine, and why they will remain a mighty medium. They are not any one thing and those that realise and harness this (limitless) potential are the artists who will take it the furthest. It took me a number of years and a barrage of rather personal criticism to see my way past what was expected, and write (yes, *express*!) for the pleasure of it.

An aspect that I reflect on with pleasure is that *Sure* began without any recognisable motives. There wasn't the remotest suggestion that I would one day make myself into a writer. In fact, it came as an absolute shock to me when I sat down at my desk (chipboard on bricks, how quaint!) and suddenly realised that I must write something. Write. This was the reason I had absconded from university, to do away with intellectual effort. This, though, would be a creative enterprise, something I had never, I repeat never, engaged in. From that first hand-written editorial (I received a great number of requests for translations) I discovered a love of writing. I adored it from that moment on.

Kane Barwick grew up in country NSW but can't seem to settle anywhere. He loves his wife, his cat and the Collingwood Magpies. He doesn't plan to stop writing any time soon.

Lachlan Musicman
In your bedroom, everyone can hear you scream

I remember my first conscious interaction with a 'zine' was in Augogo Records, the summer of 96/97. As I was flipping through the CD racks, Felicity passed me an A5 sized booklet called *How To Make Trouble and Influence People*. We were involved in radical politics at the time, so the title intrigued, and the quickly-read content appealed immediately. It was only five dollars, so I picked it up.

It's strange how these things work – I read it as soon as I arrived home, and proceeded to carry it with me for about a month to re-read over and over again. I passed it on, and over the years, I think I've bought about six copies to continuously replace the copies I was passing out to others. The content amazed me – it was 'a self improvement primer full of testimonials from numerous happy and satisfied troublemakers' and I loved every entry. Being from a conservative background, and new to radical politics I was amazed to find that while I was busy defending 'the workers' there were people out there, in Australia, advocating an 'anti-work' agenda. It totally blew my mind. The posters, stickers, anecdotes and graffiti were a total inspiration and very influential to my subsequent political development.

From there, Augogo's tiny zine rack became one of my must-see sections of the shop and I soon purchased the seminal *New Pollution*, an Australian zine anthology that came out a few months before the inaugural National Young Writers' Festival in 1997 (later to become part of the This Is Not Art Festival). I had met an amazing number of people by handing out the *How to Make Trouble* zine (in Melbourne) so that the NYWF seemed like the next stop. This is where I was suddenly thrown in the deep end – all kinds of writers on all kinds of topics. I still remember my shock when I met someone who did a 'perzine' – a zine devoted to personal writing with no explicit political notions, and it blew me away that someone could deny the political nature of zines so explicitly (what can I say, I was young and dumb).

Back in Melbourne, Polyester Books was another great source of zines and comics, as was Barricade Books on Sydney Road. Eventually I was inspired enough to do my own zine, *Amuzine* (a-monash-uni-zine, a-mu-zine etc. etc.), in time for the start of the '98 year at Monash, and continued to publish it for three more years. I was very strict about my zines – they had to be free. It cost me a lot (somewhere around $2000) but I was willing to part with that kind of money. I was very conscious

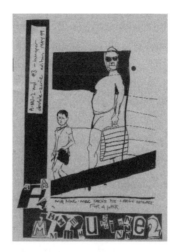

of the 'preaching to the converted' problem that many political zines fall into, so I ended up making it available only to people on campus – the content and the drive was to remedy the complete (in my mind) failings of the student rag, *Lot's Wife*. And *Lot's* was free, so I had no choice.

I loved the freedom that zines gave me. I was cutting and pasting from other zines, stealing ideas, pages, text from wherever I could find it. I could be as outrageous as I wanted to be. I was very careful to acknowledge everything that I found, and if possible, I sent a copy of the zine to all whose work I used. I loved the idea of justifying getting really stoned, sitting on my bedroom floor and creating.

I remember when I first met Sandy – he gave me a copy of one of his zines. We were in Newcastle, and went to the same uni, but had to travel interstate to meet each other. Sandy is, to me, what makes zines so great. He was a voracious reader, and an equally voracious writer. His zines made me question more than I thought was possible, he pushed the limits about what could go into print, and what shelf life they would have like no one else I know. He never kept a master copy of any of his zines – he would often cut them up to reuse parts in his next zine. His zines were simultaneously outrageous, deeply personal, and scathingly critical. The first zine of his that I was given I thought-lessly pocketed and took back to Melbourne with the other hundred or so zines I collected that year to read at my leisure. When I eventually got around to it, I opened it up, and started on the first 'article'. I don't know how to describe it, and I certainly wouldn't want people to think that I know the motivation behind it. It was a two-page first-person homoerotic S&M fantasy that involved the narrator's father and degradation. It was extremely disturbing for my (comparatively) conservative ideas of what is tasteful. It wasn't until I was bold enough to pick the zine up again three or four months later that I realised that the second story was so much more. It was another homoerotic fantasy, this time based around a 7/11 car-park late at night and the protagonist was having violent gay sex with John Howard while spouting weird mashups of communist/anti capitalist/radical rants.

As I was soon to discover, Sandy was putting these things out every month or so. They ranged from the above to just messy collage. One, that I have kept, was a study of the sun and its relation to capital. Sometimes his print run was five copies, depending on how much money he had – usually none. No one else would ever have printed any of his work, but I'm glad that Sandy did. These days he's writing a blog and a PhD, but his writing is still amazing – his years of practice have made him an excellent writer.

This is the beauty of zines to me. It isn't far removed from spending years in the garage with a guitar and amp, practice makes perfect, and only your friends will listen to your noodlings. Sometimes, though, in all the noise, you get something really special. The idea of this article, to not be about 'what is a zine', appeals for this very reason. 7U? (a fellow zine-maker) would send me parcels filled with random stuff; he worked at a photocopy centre and would send three or four zines a pack with copies of each page of each zine in multiple sizes plus added extras. Zines often come as 'packages' – a paper zine with added extras, like the time I got a scroll sent from Newcastle with a five yen piece, some random playing cards and an audio cassette. I used to do the same thing, but it was kinda random – you would just empty the 'miscellaneous drawer' of your desk into an envelope, seal it and send it across the country.

As it turned out, I thought I was the only zinester left, but I was incredibly wrong. Not only were there plenty still floating around, but the quality was still pleasingly low, on average. There's nothing better, to my mind, than a half-arsed thrown together zine – it's so raw and immediate, so rushed and honest that I really appreciate the zinesters' motivation of 'gotta get it out there, no matter the quality'.

Having said that, I'm still infinitely grateful to those that put in the effort to make something extra special – some zines are a labour of love that can last for months or years, and I appreciate the effort that has gone into them just as much. The indy- or alterna-history and 'true story' feel of *How To Make Trouble* is a great example.

How To Make Trouble and Influence People has since had countless reprintings and two sequels – *How to Stop Whining and Start Living* and *Revenge of the Troublemaker*, the last one eventually having some of my own actions in it.

At the end of my youthful, exuberant zine-making years, I had managed to acquire over a thousand zines, whatever that means; thrown in were student newspapers, and university women's publications, street press and cassette tapes.

Given the amorphous nature of the 'zine', I guess I probably was reading zines well before *How To Make Trouble* but it wasn't until then that I realised what an amazing and inspiring form of communication it could be. The total control of each individual over content, the imaginations and constructions of so many people without need for editors, target markets or advertising is such an amazing cultural asset. The tips and tricks you learn from other zinesters on how to get free photocopying, or how to distribute yourself independently, are things you can't learn by merely consuming. Once you become a producer, a writer, a collagist, an editor, you can learn so much more about how the world could and should work.

Lachlan Musicman misses making zines. He takes faith in Kylie Purr's credo that 'you don't have to put out zines to be a zinester'. He lives in Hobart where he wonders about the future of paper zines given 'the internet and blogosphere' – he favours zines because you can read them on the tram.

Lou

On the magic of mail, and the exchange of photocopied scraps

When I was a teenager I was always buying rock magazines, or reading them in the newsagency when I couldn't afford to take them home. I'd often not heard the bands, but I'd still read all about them and their world of glamour, so far from the farm where I lived and the country-town Catholic school where I spent my days.

There was one magazine, otherwise particularly forgettable, that had a couple of zine reviews in the back pages. (Had I heard of these zine things? I don't know, but it didn't  seem an odd concept at all. Just something like the homemade newspapers plucky kids kept starting in the old storybooks I'd read.) One zine mentioned was called *Barcode the World*, and just the name there caught something of what I felt about everything. So I copied down the address (and I seem to remember doing this in the shop – I was one of those customers 'This Is Not A Library' signs were made for) and sent off my two dollars and a note to some postbox.

The zine was harsh, punk and intimidating. Most importantly, it had two pages of zine reviews. And I wrote to a couple of them, and they had zines reviews, and...

It seemed like it could unfold forever, like amoebas breeding or the branching of some dysfunctional family tree. Back then (she says, switching into old-lady mode) it seemed that nearly every zine listed the addresses of others, that once you had one zine you had any number more. I was wide-eyed and enthusiastic, thrilled by these fragments of a hidden world. This world wasn't distant and glossy, but made of photocopied scraps I could make too.

The collages of newspaper headlines I made in my room late at night, obsessively cutting and pasting and reworking the news of a world that shocked and saddened me; the rants and jokes I scrawled soaked in boredom at school: I could make something. Even more important: I could give it to people. However intimidated I might have been by the urban subcultural cool of some zines, there were still spaces for me, scrappy kiddy-zines, people who seemed to be doing this thing for the same reasons I was, aggressively un-professional and happy to trade for my own small creations.

It was a cheap gift economy, a potlatch of almost worthless objects. Letters filled with beads and baubles and stickers and mixtapes and postcards and amusing news clippings and stupid ads and glitter and sequins that got everywhere. The zines were exchanged for this and amongst it, in elaborately constructed parcels that confused postal workers and parents, with stamps glued over so they could be carefully soaked off and reused.

Oh, I know nostalgia's a curse. There were always unanswered letters. I'd write away and get no reply for months, if at all, worrying that something had got lost in the mail or, worse, convincing myself that the recipient had read my letter or my zine and decided I wasn't worth replying to. And I still feel guilty about letters I know I didn't reply to and requests for zines that got lost in mess and disorganisation. And I moved to the city as soon as I could, and lost the habit of writing letters, and the relationships I had with people were never the same, when we saw each other face to face, instead of sending words and gifts back and forth.

My teenage years were dull and miserable, really, and that's fairly standard, but against this background the good things do stand out brighter. The zines themselves seem almost too flimsy to have meant so much to me. Some of the most important writing I've ever read has been in zines, that much I know, but the objects themselves are almost always too slight to hold all the meaning they're given. It was the network of zines and gifts and letters that held power – the magic in exchanging your photocopied scrawl for someone else's.

This, to me, was the point, or part of it – that, however thoughtful and personal a zine was as an individual creation, a lot of its meaning lay in the process of exchange and the connection to other zines, to the network of zines, what some people would call the 'zine community' but I think of more as something virus-like, capable of reproducing itself secretly. Killed, some might say, by exposure to the light.

I still like zines, I still read them, I still make them and swap them and send them away and I insist to my sceptical friends that they can really mean something. I try to explain that zines can mean close to everything, that they can mean something like survival. But I know I've lost some of my urgency. Maybe it's all different now that the internet's everywhere ('kids these days...' says the old lady again), but I guess I hope something like I used to be part of is still out there somewhere. A different, mutant version, of course, off the radar of arts magazines and zine fairs and self-conscious self-publishing. Hidden from nostalgic old zinesters, I hope at least some of the people who need to create and exchange find ways to do so.

Lou's zines include *Post-Consumer Waste*, *Flight Path*, and *Please to be restful*. She likes cooking, books and photocopiers. She's an anarchist and she makes terrible puns. She's working on a zine about compulsory job-search training and collaborating with the 'mutiny' collective on what they hope will become a monthly zine.

Amber Carvan
Monopoly millionaires

For me, being a Melbourne-based zine-maker in the late 1990s felt like being part of some sort of amazing art movement that you'd normally only read about in back issues of hip British magazines.

I was working in Fitzroy at the time so I had the luxury of being able to wander into Polyester Books during my lunch hour and peruse all the latest zine offerings. I was smitten. Personal style zines and mini-comics were just starting to boom and that was exactly the sort of thing that captivated me. I loved the idea of getting to know someone through their zine, and particularly that delicious irony that it's often easier to be open and honest with complete strangers than with your closest friends. I found myself being more creative and productive than ever before. Making zines led to meeting other creators and before long almost all my friends were fellow zine-makers. I met my partner, Richard, through zines — a relationship that has long outlasted the environment from which it was born.

MILK BAR/RACING CAR – Five of your dollars – wherever you're from.

Milk Bar

The '90s zine explosion was definitely a phenomenon of place and time. The creative energy was palpable. Richard and I would collect mountains of correspondence from our PO box every week — letters and zines from friends and strangers all over the world. There were 24-hour comic jams, zine parties, writers were collaborating, anybody with a creative bone in their body (and many without) made zines.

Sure enough, the network of Melbourne zine-makers, which was already significant, began to get properly organised. This new level of organisation spawned a friendly competition between zine-makers and before long we were smack bang in the middle of a movement of genuinely creative and passionate individuals, bouncing ideas off each other, upping the ante with every new issue when it came to productivity and production values.

Milkbar emerged as a direct result of this zine boom. At a very simple level, Richard and I felt genuinely overawed by some of the small press being churned out at that time and we wanted to share the zines we loved with as many people as possible. Deeper down (and no doubt inspired by our own creative aspirations) we wanted zines to be appreciated beyond the safe confines of the scene within which they were created. Ultimately, we wanted to inspire zine-makers to take on the mainstream arts world. We felt quite strongly that zine-making was an art form, and that if more zine-makers thought of themselves as artists, and exposed themselves to the same rigours that budding young artists do, then youth arts in Australia would be much more vibrant and exciting.

We came up with the idea of *Milkbar* – an intelligent and professional journal that would treat the Australian zine scene as a movement and discuss it critically and thoughtfully.

We set to work at the kitchen table in the evenings, after we knocked off from our day jobs, and seconded friends and fellow zine-makers to contribute artwork and articles and to write reviews for no money. The first issue of *Milkbar* was published in 1998 and we were pleased with the result – chunky, small format, burst bound, desktop published, professionally printed…no cut and paste in sight. Content-wise it was roughly half zine/comic reviews and half articles/comics/fiction. (An inspiration was Jeff Levine's *Destroy All Comics* which, coincidentally, also folded after a small number of issues and left Jeff feeling despondent and regretful.)

All in all *Milkbar* received a great deal of support and praise both inside and outside the zine community but much of this was overshadowed by vitriolic criticism from a small but vocal number of zine-makers. Our desire to give zines a greater exposure was perceived by some as an attempt to 'mainstream' zines and was fiercely resisted. In hindsight, the fact that this took us completely by surprise is testimony to our naivety.

In particular, the zine reviews included in *Milkbar* were the subject of heated debate. Our desire to expose zines to the same degree of scrutiny as other art forms in the public domain proved to be a little too confronting for a community that had previously been sheltered from any degree of public criticism or comment.

Before long it became apparent to us that the zine scene suffers from the same crippling self-consciousness as the alternative music movement. From the insistence that the 'fringe' nature of a zine is integral to the form of media, it follows that zines by definition lose credibility with popularity. A successful zine is anathema. What a horrible fate for such an authentic and thoroughly appealing art form!

We weren't at all sentimental about our decision to stop publishing *Milkbar* after just two issues. It seemed logical to invest our time, energy and money into our own art, rather than sinking it into showcasing the work of people who didn't seem to want to be show-cased.

It's interesting to note that the handful of zine creators (mostly comic artists) who opted to think of themselves as 'artists' rather than 'zine-makers' have gone on to achieve many exciting things in the youth arts arena – holding group and solo exhibitions, working on innovative projects with arts festivals such as Noise and Next Wave, and receiving funding from state and federal agencies to create new work.

For me, working with young creators who are happy to be considered 'artists' and who are excited (rather than horrified) at the prospect of mainstream media exposure has proven to be a much more rewarding experience – professionally and personally.

Though the boom has long since gone Richard and I remain zine lovers through and through. We've never entertained the possibility of reviving *Milkbar* though – we're resigned to the fact that, as an art form, zines are well and truly doomed. The currency in circulation within the zine scene is completely different to that used in the wider arts community. It's like monopoly money. Zine-makers who want to create meaningful and innovative 'art' must first escape from the confines of zine-dom, because outside of the zine community their money is pretty much worthless.

Amber Carvan works as an editor and producer. She lives in the Blue Mountains with her mother, partner, two children and a sizeable collection of small dogs.

Vanessa Berry
A journey into deepest, darkest detail

Imagine writing one day and including everything, following every thought to its end.

Initially this wasn't what I intended to do. In 1997 I was part of a project in which a group of zine-writers posted something to each other at the beginning of every month. I chose this particular something by chance. The first of my 23rds was an inauspicious day where I was at home waiting for a lady to come and look at a pram my mother had advertised in the *Trading Post*. Thinking of what I could make for the project, I used the blank afternoon to devise a kind of extended postcard of my day. I called it *Laughter and the Sound of Teacups*, a name chosen by opening the book I was reading (Philip Larkin's *Jill*) and poking my finger onto a random line. I was nineteen years old. If anyone had called me a writer I would have scoffed.

As these beginnings suggest, *Latsot* (its pleasingly snappy abbreviated title) relied on the unconscious and the instinctual. I didn't pause to examine motives or consequences, or to question whether anyone would want to read about my life. I just assumed people would, because the everyday life of strangers was the kind of thing that I found interesting.

The mail exchange project faltered, but the zine firmly established itself as part of my life. I enjoyed the focus it gave me, the mechanical pleasure of regular photocopying and posting and the feeling of connection that came with releasing it for people to read.

At the time I was living in a crumbling palace of a house, walls stuck all over with pictures, drawings, quotes, newspaper headlines, shopping lists. I aimed to make the space around me reflect the space inside my head; both were cluttered. I was an eccentric, over-thinking, early-twenties housewife, with a lot of time to dream.

Laughter and the Sound of Teacups couldn't have existed in any other way but as a zine. Zines were maps of possibilities and making them I felt bold and important. Their energy came from the fact they could be utterly silly or utterly morbid – they could be anything. They were epic and heartfelt, an honest reflection of their creators' desires.

I used my zine to celebrate minutiae, the kinds of things that are only remembered in the moment, before being lost beneath the surge of the present. I wanted *Latsot* to act as a net for thoughts, capturing the twists and wisps that curled through my mind on any day. When I read *The Mezzanine* by Nicholson Baker, I understood his desire to quantify thought, to record everything; it spurred me on further. I challenged myself to see how deeply I could go into detail, how accurately I could chart twenty-four hours.

So, after the early light-hearted sketches, the issues became increasingly eidetic in their detail. After every 23rd I'd write a chain of notes, which I would later reconstitute into the long story of what happened to me that day. I worked hard to remember everything so I wouldn't have to interrupt the day itself with note-taking, training my memory so I could turn it off and on at will. Turning on my memory meant that I was able to remember pretty much everything that happened. I would mentally build a great, cumbersome necklace, where each unit of thought suggested the next. I could embed thoughts in my mind like poking smarties into cupcake icing.

I wanted to illuminate every moment, make drama out of the everyday. Although I kept it a secret and never wrote about it directly, my life at that time was limited by illness. I didn't have experiences which I felt stood up to the scrutiny of relatives and old high school rivals or to the 'What do you do?' death knell; things like overseas travel, a stunning university career, involvement in community organisations. But if I could write about LCD displays, taxi-drivers and toast as if they were defining, it didn't matter that they were just little things.

However at the time I made no such justifications, and describing the project as a kind of self-becoming feels reductive now.

I wrote every issue passionately. I was diving deeper into a love affair with details and I wanted to take other people with me. I wasn't focused on self-revelation. Although it seemed like I was giving the reader license to crawl into my skin for a day, I was more of a frame people could peek through than a picture to be examined.

It was impossible for me to live a 23rd exactly as if it were just any other day. Everything was heightened, anticipating memorial-isation. I could feel a nebulous net of people around me, the hundred sets of eyes that would later skim over the description of my failure to make *pan de muerto* or my reminiscence on what band T-shirts I owned as a teenager. This was a glorious feeling, knowing that the day would be trapped and inspected. I felt spotlit, golden, like each 23rd was my birthday. It gave me the same feeling of secret pleasure.

Each issue was a letter, to everyone and no one in particular, written with love. Which is why, for a long time, I didn't really consider it as writing. For me writing was about premeditation and crafting. *Laughter and the Sound of Teacups* was more like a museum display. It came from the collector part of me, the child who liked to put paint sample cards in order and spent car journeys counting the number and type of squashed cans she saw on the roadside.

By 2002 I'd been writing fiction for a while, considering its important building blocks. The 23rds were still gushing forth, longer and more detailed than ever (hitting the summit of 14,500 words in January), but rather than a collection of field notes, I began to consider them as pieces of writing.

I am not trying to suggest that writing involuntarily is more noble or honest or effective than writing as a considered practice, but when I found myself automatically clicking into my *Latsot* 'style' and wondering about my impact as a character, I realised it was time to stop.

I no longer wanted to say everything, indeed I felt I was drowning in detail. With every issue I wrote I knew I could have gone further, said more. Whilst this challenge had excited me, it became increasingly remote from what I was interested in. I had crafted a particular way of seeing and awareness of thought through the 23rds, but I felt I had come to a point where my apprenticeship was over. I had wrestled with detail and now I wanted to retreat and think about different ways I could write, using what I had learnt. So, abruptly, I sent death notices to everyone on my mailing list:

I feel that I have written *Laughter and the Sound of Teacups* for long enough. Sixty-seven of them exist, I look at them and feel heavy from all the details and ideas contained within. I think that if I don't end it now, they will become hackneyed, and I don't want to cling onto the concept as if writing about my life is more important than my life itself.

It has been difficult to think of a good way to end this. I liked the idea of one final grand day, summing up all I have achieved over the last five and a half years, drawing all the themes together neatly. This is how life works in fiction, but despite how much of a character I may seem in my writing, I am a real-life girl with many things I still wouldn't share with anybody. I couldn't think of a good way to sum everything up, because I would have to step outside of myself and view things as if I were a character, and all the days in between each 23rd were a shadowy waiting period before the one illuminated twenty-four hours.

Even now on 23rds I feel uncomfortable flutters that there is something I should be doing, a nervous rush like being out and suddenly suspecting I forgot to turn off the oven (a topic I wrote about, at length, in at least five issues of *Laughter and the Sound of Teacups*). Sometimes I miss the illuminated feeling like I miss the touch of an old love to whom I cannot return.

Vanessa Berry is a zinemaker and writer of experimental non-fiction. Her current zine is *I am a Camera*. See http://www.vanessaberryworld.com

Michael Farrell

The Wild, the Innocent, and the Kierkegaard Shuffle

Michael Farrell is
researching
improvisation and
Australian culture at
Deakin University. His
collection of poems *ode
ode* was published by
Salt in 2003.

There are those who want to know how things are on earth:
this story is for them.

Sven Hesse, through birth or bad luck – you choose which – was one
of the guilty. The guilty are responsible for all the shit that happens.
Maybe he never killed anyone, but if there are two suspects, and the
other one is innocent, then the guilty suspect goes to gaol. Despite all
their time there, and the homosexuality rife among the guilty population,
they manage to increase. The crime rate's pretty stable actually. But
more and more gaols are built all the time. Sven had avoided gaol so far,
at least he'd only visited his relatives and lovers there.

He spent a lot of time on the streets too. Busking mostly. And
whenever the cops drove by he'd break out into a Springsteen song
guaranteed to make a blue boy cry.

He came out of Hoboken
He'd always thought he was innocent
He'd never known what bent cop meant

He never wanted to hurt no-one
...Now he had he was broken
('He Came Out of Hoboken')

The cops were all innocent these days, by law. But as long as Sven could appeal to their sentimentality, he thought they – and all of us – had a chance. Speaking of sentimentality, what did clichés like 'a chance' mean? Even if you could ask him, he'd probably just sing some Springsteen song at you. That was just a gag too. He had a story that after the last oil war, after Springsteen died in suspiciously Elvis-like circumstances, that some tapes had surfaced: his late, great and last work. The officials at Bruceland have always denied there was any late work, apart from the versions of gospel songs that sold like hot candles when everyone – guilty and innocent alike – thought they could be living the last days. Maybe the songs exist, and maybe they don't, but the songs Sven sang were all written by himself (meaning the actual words had never been sung before, but I guess the Boss had a hand in it, he sang the words into Sven's head, and into being).

The guilty often write great songs, but except for a few decades last century, they've never had recording contracts. Unless you count women like Carla. She had what's known as a gender exemption; she'd made an oath of allegiance to the patriarchy, because as every woman knows, 'it's the only way you can work in this town'. So even though Carla Sympatico was actually black, and wrote her own songs most of the time, she had a contract and enough sentimentality to like the idea of recording something by one of the guilty. And what was notable about her was her refusal to take credit *as a singer*, for writing her own songs. She was proud of them, but she said, give me credit as a writer for those songs, not as a singer, singing's all in the performance, and if someone can sing them better than me, give them the credit, even if they don't write their own, and don't say I'm better than someone who doesn't...you can't compare a writer to someone who doesn't write, you can only compare our singing. That was without getting her started on comparing different styles of singing as if one was better than another.

She said some styles *may be* more rooted to truth or to the heart, but in the scheme of things, all songs, all styles fed off one another, and we all need different things at different times. Carla was the closest thing we had to Madonna, and even if she'd never say she thought the leader was brilliant, she had made that oath. A woman of contradictions? Isn't that just another cliché? Anyone of more than two dimensions has contradictions – and this is just a construction of a brief period of time. If you need further reassurance imagine her future career when she finally decides to stop identifying with the idea of 'city girl' and moves to the bush and joins the insurrectionists.

City girl, you wear your curly hair down
Cause there aint enough technology in this town
To keep it upNot without restraint
You've been there
You've got your hair-story...
('Hair Story Pt. 1')

Innocents have expectations. They are .6 protestant, have a .6 income rating, are .8 white. They have always existed, at least it seems that way. They have been known under other names, but 'innocents' now seems inevitable. The name came from a follower, or as those without a voice might say, a perverter of Kierkegaard. Kierkegaard proposed that abstract thought was thought without a thinker, thought without an ethical dimension. Greg Jinton-Jones developed a theory of the abstract crime, or the crime without a criminal. In a radical and popular move he conceived of crime without an ethical dimension! This meant that what used to be known as white-collar crime was now seen as not criminal at all because the so-called crimes hadn't been committed by criminals. Everyone knew what a criminal was like, and what the crimes that gave them their name were. And if they hadn't actually committed a crime, statistics, not to mention common sense, proved that they soon would if not prevented. Massive pardons of those from innocent backgrounds were enthusiastically given by the current leader, and pre-emptive gaoling measures were introduced, ensuring that the five per cent of the population deemed most likely to commit crime i.e. those who were now known as criminals were kept locked away. Plans to increase this percentage were under way. Meanwhile various legislative and linguistic measures were also under way to divide the innocent from the guilty.

Protests by women were effectively silenced by threats to include all women under guilty legislation. The leader's wife, or leaderess, showed by example by taking the first public oath of allegiance to the patriarchy ('upholder of innocence'). All women in senior positions, followed by all women in government jobs, and eventually all women in all jobs, were required to take the oath and recant any former feminist beliefs and beg pardon for any actions made in the name of feminism. Abortion had long been illegal by then, in what became known as the innocent world. Equal pay was a dead issue, as pay became based on an individual's innocence rating. This meant that White Christmas Records, Carla Sympatico's label, kept most of her earnings as she had a relatively low innocence rating. Her rating was boosted however by her earning power and celebrity status; TV time having, as ever, a 'whitewashing' effect.

Sven and Carla had an affair, which Sven's friends were split in advising in favour of and against. The against friends felt vindicated, because the affair didn't last, and she didn't cover any of his songs. But Sven was happy, he'd never had a lover like Carla before, and he was thrilled by the stardom she did give him: she wrote a song about him. 'I Looked in The Mirror (Sven, The Two of Us)' was a minor hit, and was the closest Carla would get to writing a protest song.

He was wilder than my hair had ever been
When he was mine we were both non-scene
He had two left feet
& he led me a dance
I wasn't thinking of the final circumstance
I left it to chance
I left him to chance
I looked in the mirror
& saw the glass

One critic suggested that she was indicating a move away from 'hair: her great theme', another the unlikely notion that she'd been immersing herself in early Springsteen. Sven's popularity increased after that, and he lost his anxiety of influence. His Boss tapes spiel had been invented partly to pre-empt those who might call him derivative (for though the buskers and other guilty artists may not have contracts or a press devoted to their art forms, the oral review was a strong and sometimes savage force). Now he thought of himself as a prophet, an interpreter, a true believer. He wrote a song about Carla too.

You made me honest
(Want to run to the trees)
You made me realise what innocence really means
Now I've come to the end of my string
Will I find a way to keep on going?
You were my expectation
(and what do I know about trees?)
('Unpaid Night (Carla – The Two of Us)')

Kierkegaard's name signified little more than a sentimental token, and an occasional stamp subject when the leader felt restless about his own appearance. The government wasn't scared of the association, because they didn't care what Kierkegaard really wrote, and were certain that mere ideas could never harm them. The innocent strategies of denial, censorship, repression – and if necessary, torture and murder – were their reserve after all. No one studied philosophy any more: it wasn't fashionable or available.

The lives of the innocents: what's to tell? Their stories are the story of the culture, the structure that makes the guilty what they are. Of course the innocent are sometimes victims, which makes them guilty, in a way. Innocent victims of violent crime and sometimes suicide; more often they join the leader's faceless Anti-Force. To be honest, that's about all I know. Greg Jinton-Jones's story is the predictable one of an instigator: he has a secret. He's gay, or has a Jewish mother or wife, he used to be an abortionist, he used to love animals or plants.

Now he drinks and or takes drugs and or gambles in a desperate effort to forget – and as a way of expressing his joy at being one of the power-ful. He might actually think the word 'joy' when he's doing it.

How wild was Sven Hesse? Was there more to him than a negative reflection? He began to build on what he thought of as his 'inheri-tance'. He began to use what the insurrectionists thought of as tainted ideas, that is, those of Kierkegaard. He began to talk about his 'war songs', though officially it was a time of peace. This was the last song he sang before he left town, some say he joined the insurrectionists, others that he had too many unpaid bills.

High up in a plane looking for something to bomb
Lying in a field with my foot blown off
I can't escape those abstract thoughts
Can't escape those abstract thoughts
Rotting in prison since I was twenty-five
Drive a taxi all night when I should be retired
The radio the TV blasting at me
Abstract thoughts
Abstract thoughts
I can't escape those abstract thoughts
('Abstract Me Out of Here')

He sang this song out into the ether; and now you, the representatives, the embodiment of the ether have come, as the guilty have hoped and prayed, to do something about it.

Kate Middleton

Essay on Absence – Journal (with Judy Garland)

for Joanne Currie

I haven't really seen it, Caravaggio's

Death of…but the saint holds his neck

with his right hand, his forehead

with the left

and it really is the dumbfoundedness of mourning.

(He shows the Virgin dead.

'Bonne Nuit, Judy Garland'

the papers in Montreal read.)

They feel flogged by it,

their grief, and I suppose it's true

no-one cares about propriety, anymore.

(It's already heretical that she has died,

and no-one cares about her body, bloated

and dishevelled.) It is her lack

hung on a wall,

but all I saw was coloured light.

———

Gunmetal and lonesome blue. These words

to describe the sky, July. I would have just said

leaden – my mother
through a telephone. Darkening I said,
and it was there, too, a complicity

in the sun's stiff resolve to fall on its own sword
before rising again. (The New, new Garland,
the papers once heralded her.) Then it broke.

You wished you were elsewhere (in the country
you said) where the sky wasn't stained.

(You wanted to see the stars.)

————

I always thought there was something sad
in Judy's smile and her diminished body,
breasts bound
playing little Dorothy. She arrived

with her dad and the first neon sign in Lancaster,
California, at the age of two

and later sang Zing! went the strings of my heart
to him through the radio

a dutiful choked up electrified songbird

as he died – spinal meningitis, diagnosed
a few hours before the end.

————

Before there were baths
there were not baths. I was scalded by dirt
and could string it out for days.

Cleanliness came later, and unfledged anger, too.
The dirt is something forgotten.

Her #1 fan failed to record it
in his shrine to her. It only records
the hours that shine, he said.

The dirt leaves a scar like your voice:
do you have get here what are you so stop

———

There should be something voluptuous,
rubato and full-bodied. Something
time could betray in a hiccup. Something

with the froth of manicures and minor catastrophes.

There should be more parts
satin and purple. Lana's nice, Judy said

but talking to her is like talking
to a beautiful vase. There should be a boozy clarinet.

———

She only managed 68 pages of her life
before she realised she'd rather die

than set it all out. You once said

the visible and the invisible imply each other.

I've written lists, inventories, explanations,
here they are.
Twenty-three lines blank.

———

I have a friend who plays flute
as if it were a prelude to judgement.

When she sees something beautiful
she jumps and screams
it's so damn beautiful

as though she's going to cry because she can't
take it in, the blade of it. Judy's scrapbook

records the story of a girl
bitten to death by black widow spiders
nesting in her beehive hairdo,

When the notes sound there is the scent
of 3 a.m. hanging at their centre. When
she cries she refers to the time

Kate Middleton is a Melbourne writer. Her work has been published in
many Australian journals and newspapers.

Adrian Martin

Point of No Return

Wong Kar-wai's 2046

Adrian Martin is a
freelance film critic, and
Co-Editor of ROUGE
(www.rouge.com.au).
His forthcoming books
are on Terrence Malick
and Brian De Palma.

In an era when every gung-ho scriptwriting manual tells aspiring filmmakers to *drive their stories forward*, Hollywood-style, at any cost, there has appeared on the world stage a special group of movies that resist simply by staying (in narrative terms) in one spot. They are not merely films in which, whimsically, 'nothing happens' (as the *Seinfeld*-derived saying goes), but films about the real and agonising *difficulty of moving forward* – a syndrome that afflicts, all at once, the characters in these stories, the world they represent, and the entire 'machine' of narrative cinema. Not surprisingly, these films most often end up being about a kind of repetition-compulsion: going over the same ground, turning in a circle, unable to break free.

Hou Hsiao-hsien's *Millennium Mambo* (2001) – one of the least immediately acclaimed films of this great Taiwanese director – set the going-around-in-a-circle pattern of recent years. It is, at its most banal level (and many viewers and critics could see nothing beyond the banality), the story of a poor, young woman, Vicky (Shu Qi), who cannot break free of her bad, abusive relationship with a highly possessive DJ, Hao-hao (Tuan Chun-hao). Hou does not puff this story up to any tragic or majestic plane. The characters remain shallow, almost behaving on autopilot.

Their world of music and clubs and clothes is set at a low level of constant sensory stimulation. Hou's camera drifts, often very close to the action, over fields of colour, shiny detail, obscure zones of shadow and obstruction; abstraction calls at every moment. Both the content and the form express a kind of niggling, suffocating, finally unbearable kind of stasis: nothing is driving forward, everything and everybody is being slowly worn down by repetition and compulsion (captured especially in Hao-hao's relentless interrogations of where Vicky has been, who she has spoken to, what she is thinking…). The film begins with an extraordinary time-warp tableau that opens a loop never to be closed: we see Vicky walking along a public tunnel-passageway, enjoying her own bodily gestures (as Hou enjoys them, in slow motion, following behind with his camera) – and we hear a voice from the future, Vicky ten years hence, from the place where she is free, but still a little haunted by the thought that Hao-hao may be, effectively, in the place of that camera, tracking, watching, spying…

Getting to that future – to that almost sci-fi 'off-screen space' inhabited by a plaintive voice – is what is so difficult, and *Millennium Mambo* isn't going to make the passage to that act any easier, for Vicky or for us. Hou's concerns recur in another masterpiece of recent years that is unlikely to reach Australia's 'boutique' art houses: Philippe Garrel's memoir of 1968 and what came after, *Les Amants réguliers* (*Ordinary Lovers*, 2005). The film begins directly with that 'crack in reality' (as Jean Eustache called it in his *The Mother and the Whore*, 1973): the riots and struggles of May '68 that turned Paris into an 'occupied zone', anticipating, in its chaos, the war-torn cities and fields of so many conflicts to follow…As police assemble, Garrel inserts on the soundtrack a slogan from one of his young, romantic, impossibly beautiful revolutionaries (one of whom is played by the director's own son, Louis Garrel): 'Enough of repetition. Move forward!'

The English subtitler made a curious choice here, because *répétition* probably means, in this context, 'rehearsal' – but the literal translation is just as resonant. Because, the moment that the 'crack' seals up – the very morning after, in fact, in Garrel's unreal but poetic conceit – the characters become mired in repetition (they 'lose the revolution indoors', as one cynic says of them), trying desperately to find the spark (in love, in drugs, in books, in art, in music, in words, in dance) that will enable them to go on living from day to day, in history, as now 'ordinary lovers'...One hour of revolution, two hours of everyday life (that's the structure of the film), an unhappy ending: how does anybody or anything move forward? There's not even the tiniest hinge into the future, like in that exceptional black comedy of neurotic repetition-compulsion, Paul Thomas Anderson's *Punch-Drunk Love* (2002) where, after all the agony, the final line offers what is, in effect, an opening line, the start of a story at last: 'Here we go.'

Wong Kar-wai's *2046* (2004) also boasts an inventive way of framing a story in which nothing moves forward easily. In a flurry at its beginning, we see glimpses of the personal life of the hero, Chow Mo-wan (Tony Leung), mixed up with volleys of the extravagant sci-fi tale he is writing. That tale – which is also called *2046* – is about a journey to somewhere that is, ambiguously, both a time and a place, time *as* a place or location: the world of 2046, where 'lost memories' can be retrieved, where answers can be found, where unfinished business can at last be closed. But even this seeming Shangri-la offers, not really a new start, but only a renovated kind of stasis: in 2046, we are informed (and it is a terse allusion, beyond the film, to the future fate of Hong Kong), 'nothing will change anymore'. As we observe the hip protagonist of this film-within-the-film (played by Takuya Kimura), we hear him reflect that nobody knows whether 2046 indeed holds the key to all these recovered riches, since 'nobody has ever returned' – but then he adds the tantalising rider, 'except me'. What a beautiful 'fold' with which to begin a story!

But where does this fold go, to where does it lead, exactly? Wong Kar-wai folds it up again, slowly, painstakingly: in the course of the film, we will pass from the fantasy of the time traveller – who never will manage to tell us the 'truth' about 2046, of course – to the fantasist, the author himself, Mo-wan. His character is his *alter ego*, the guy who can do in a story what the author cannot do in real life. He flatters himself by finally taking over his character's futuristic narration. But Mo-wan does not, cannot move forward; everything is draining away from him, leaving only a melancholic after-image – even the memory of his time with Lai-chen (Maggie Cheung), reprised from Wong's previous *In the Mood for Love* (2000), ends with the apparition of him alone, slumped in

the same position in the same cab, but without her. So that, in the closing moments of the film, when Mo-wan utters the words of his
imaginary hero – 'no one has ever returned' – this time there is no fold,
no hinge, no exception. Only the point of no return.

How to retell the plot of *2046* – so full of incident, so rich with
character, with the historical succession of times and places, and yet so
amorphous and inconclusive? We see a man with a parade of women – of
different types, different ages. Every viewer might diagnose his erotic-
romantic pathology differently, locating its centre in one woman or
another: maybe it's Lai-chen, who is absent, or maybe it's Jingwen (Faye
Wong), who chooses another, or Bai Ling (Zhang Ziyi) who implodes in
her non-stop party-girl manner, or maybe it's any of these women he toys
with and rejects and then laments…In the theatre of Mo-wan's melancholy, both repetition and compulsion (and the death-drive that, for
Freud, they both portend) are at work: he is in the business of inventing
'lost objects', both in his art and in his life, and fetishising their memory.

At its high point, the film gives us a sequence that perfectly
captures Mo-wan's stasis. Wong Kar-wai is well known as a writer-direc-
tor-auteur who chews up everything he sees and reads before and during
the production of his works: as well as Liu Yichang's 1962 novel *The
Drunkard* (which supplies several of the literary intertitles that punctu-
ate the film), I also think that Wong had Leonard Cohen's song 'Last
Year's Man' (from *Songs of Love and Hate*, 1971) in mind when he fash-
ioned this sequence. Cohen's song is about a writer, and the act of
writing: he sits down to begin, and then all the imaginings, the possible
scenarios pour forth…But the portrait is not one of unfettered creativity,
quite the opposite: the song thuds to a close with the revelation that, for
this writer, 'an hour has gone by, and he has not moved his hand'. It's
writer's block as an existential condition. Wong pictures this quite literally: Mo-wan's pen poised above a sheet of paper, as the hours (one, ten,
a hundred) flee. The image is instantly taken up and expanded, grandil-
oquently, in outer space, where the cyber-Jingwen (caught in that eternal
delay between an android's actions and her emotional reactions) stands
and looks out a window, for one, ten, a hundred years…'The rain falls
down on the works of last year's man' – Cohen's words could be not only
an epitaph, but literally an image from, *2046*.

Like the vivid fragments and aphorisms that constitute Roland Barthes' *A Lover's Discourse*, Wong's vignettes of longing and loss elicit an intense emotional identification on the part of sympathetic viewers (and complete, almost phobic rejection from unsympathetic ones) – an identification less with the characters and their fictive biographies than with lyrically condensed states, moods and situations from the Book of Love: snapshots of desire, betrayal, separation. Earlier filmmakers achieved immortal flashes of this kind, of 'transpersonal' evocations of love – Ingmar Bergman in *Summer with Monika* (1953), Jean-Luc Godard in *Bande à part* (1964) – but it took Wong's marriage of this dream to the multi-plot/multi-character form (initially in *Days of Being Wild*, 1990) to make it a sustained, extended reality.

However, this identification is also a trap for analysts and fans alike. It encourages commentators to speak of the films as if they were only primers on modern love – the cool detachment, the inability to commit, the serial liaisons, the pangs of nostalgic regret – as if the characters were as real and deep as we (hope we) are, complete with personal histories and destinies extending well beyond the limits of the film (an illusion that Wong stokes by 'carrying over' some characters from one film to another). As a result it is easy to discuss any Wong film at great length without ever really touching the remarkable intricacy of its formal and stylistic procedures – a tendency that Sylvia Lawson once described as 'managing to overlook the fact that films are made up of images and sounds'.

In this respect the majority of commentaries on Wong's films simply carry on the standard business of criticism in the narrative arts: they install the imaginary, three-dimensional lives of fictional beings at the top of the aesthetic hierarchy, and proceed to speculate on the inner motivations, intentions and drives that give rise to their dramatic behaviour, finally arriving at some moral evaluation of that behaviour. This is roughly what we call 'humanism' in arts criticism and, to a large extent, it deserves the instant bad press it gets in some quarters – perhaps because it continues to rule the way that most people learn, practice or absorb the business of criticism on a day-to-day basis: to talk about a film is to talk about its characters (and how well, how realistically or believably, the actors brought them to life). Yet such humanism will only get us so far, and no further, into Wong's films. The characters in *2046* are less 'real people' than vivid *figures*, emblems of certain 'forms of being' (to borrow the title of a recent valuable book by Leo Bersani and Ulysse Dutoit): they represent different ways of inhabiting time (past, present or future), of living in the mirror of others or within oneself, of acknowledging or disavowing the lessons of experience.

The elasticity of these emblematic character-figures is best seen in the film's unique treatment of the theme of ageing. Age is rarely explicitly mentioned, but is an omnipresent motif. The women cover a large span of years, from Lulu (Carina Lau) down to Jingwen's pubescent sister. And Mo-wan as he is in the 1960s, embodied by the charismatic Leung, has appeared not only five years previously in *In the Mood for Love*, but a full decade again before that, in the enigmatic ending (another surprise 'fold' that seems to kick off an entirely different story) of *Days of Being Wild*. So Leung visibly ages, in reality, from film to film, while his character remains stuck in time: a striking cinematic paradox of the kind that Wong loves to cultivate, and a superb response to the fragile illusion entertained by Mo-wan that things 'will never change'.

But what of the images and sounds in *2046* – not only the inspired collage of musical selections but also the dense 'sound design' of voices, noises and atmospheres which serves to whisk us in and out of the film's many zones and environments? In one of finest texts in the annals of film criticism, Jean-André Fieschi in 1973 retrospectively hailed F.W. Murnau's classic horror film *Nosferatu* (1922) as marking the moment – another point of no return – at which 'the modern cinema was born', because its 'plastic, rhythmic and narrative elements are no longer graded in importance, but in strict interdependence upon each other'. Today, Wong Kar-wai is the cinema's most advanced plastician working outside the hothouse laboratory of the avant-garde. From his first feature, *As Tears Go By* in 1988, he began experimenting with variations in the speed of the image – although, at the beginning, his stylistic ambition could have been mistaken for the same old, clichéd recourse to slow motion for instants of high drama, urban ambience or lyrical death. At the outset of his collaboration with cinematographer Chris Doyle (an Australian expatriate), in films including *Chungking Express* (1995) and *Fallen Angels* (1996), his repertoire of technical experiments expanded: colour and light were subject to all manner of tinkering (strobe, sepia, saturation), the camera became radically mobile in Doyle's hands and, as a post-produced object, the image became fragmented and multiplied, comparing within the one frame the fast-motion of streaking city lights with the slow-motion of a strung-out character.

2046 – during the production of which Wong and Doyle ceased (at least for the time being) their collaboration, and Kwan Pung-leung and Lai Yiu-fai stepped in – inaugurates a new phase in the director's mastery of plasticity. The mobile camera has been replaced by largely static compositions, and Wong has evolved an elaborate set of pictorial strategies. Since much of the film is shot in disorienting close-up, heads loom in space, making it often impossible for us to place or reconstruct the precise layout of settings. Vast areas of the frame are regularly blacked out, whether by darkened objects or by bodies placed in the foreground, or by various kinds of post-production treatment – many shots look like they are have been frozen in the middle of an old-fashioned screen 'wipe'. The co-ordination of colour in costume and decor, handled by Alfred Yau and Wong's close, regular collaborator William Chang, is taken to new heights of lyrical delirium. The extreme edges of the frame are constantly in use, decentring gestures and events. The human body – especially the face – is subject to subtle deformations that quietly suggest the paintings of Francis Bacon, as in this typical shot/reverse shot volley:

Such literal 'figuration' in the plastic sense allows us to find a way back to the characters as themselves figures – literally pieces of a composition – rather than three-dimensional beings. In his Murnau essay, Fieschi notes that 'it is as though each character had his own rhythm of movement, his own personal (and habitual) way of occupying space, and turning his passage into a tangible trace of joy, terror or menace.' Wong, within his own art, applies this principle

systematically. Look at how the characters – particularly the women – are each given their 'own' signature place in the frame to inhabit from one moment and situation to the next, even if it means completely twisting the mise en scène (the staging and positioning of the actors in the set) every which way to accommodate this parti pris:

The relationships between characters are rendered in an equally plastic way. Working closely with his editor (William Chang again), Wong turns *2046* into the endlessly varied drama of a single, central idea: the 'tearing away' of bodies that try, sometimes violently, to make contact. Here, the elaborate shot compositions mesh with the highest powers of montage: few films give such gravity to the separation between bodies inscribed in the interval between a shot and its reverse shot during exchanges of dialogue. But it is in the flurries of fragmented detail that this drama of tearing becomes most dramatic: the moments of contact – such as the passing of an object between hands – are like explosions of action, dances around an impossible fusion. And such fumbled moments are always followed by strict rhymes that set the characters back into their own spaces and rhythms, separated by a vast interval, such as in this moment when Su Lizhen (Gong Li) parts from Mo-wan:

ADRIAN MARTIN

Almost inevitably, Wong has been accused of being a filmmaker who, in the worst possible sense, lingers in the past and cannot move on. With its fulsome references to his previous films, *2046* is taken by some as a backward-looking wallow, an anthology of Wong's own mannerisms, nothing new, the work of last year's man. As in the case of Terrence Malick, the fact that Wong discovers his films 'in process' – exploring, revising, discarding and condensing many characters, plot threads, situations and scenarios along the way – raises the suspicion, among those with an unquestioned adherence to 'industry standards of professionalism', that he is only ever playing around, hiding the truth that he has nothing to say. This leads to a comment like that of HK cinema expert Stephen Teo (author of the otherwise indispensable *Wong Kar-wai: Auteur of Time*) that *2046* 'covers no new ground in style or narrative'. Indeed, Wong has reached a point of no return in his career with this magisterial achievement; from now on, he has committed himself to what Jean-Luc Godard (in his *Histoire(s) du cinéma*) called the 'cinematograph', which is 'very precisely, a form which thinks'.

Ingrid Wassenaar

Whatever

The Films of Laurent Cantet and Robert Guédiguian

Ingrid Wassenaar is a
former Fellow of Christ's
College Cambridge and
a University Lecturer in
the French Department
there. Her publications
include *Proustian
Passions* (OUP, 2000).
She is currently an
Honorary Lecturer in the
French Department at
Sydney University.

psuchê pasa pantos epimeleitai tou apsuchou
('All soul has the care of all that is soulless', Plato, *Phaedrus*, 246b6)

*Attempts to justify Russell Crowe's assault on the night desk clerk at the
Mercer Hotel last month came up short around here. Everyone sided with the
humble clerk…but that is only if you ignore (as Crowe could not) what Josh
(full name Nestor Estrada) muttered to him on the phone. What Josh said
was 'Whatever'.*
Nick Paumgarten, 'Fighting Words: Whatever,' *New Yorker*, 11 July 2005

Why is 'Whatever' cause for clerk-bashing? Somehow that single
word speaks to us all, and explains – if it doesn't justify – Russell
Crowe's furious assault. 'Whatever' speaks to us about contempt,
about apathy, a refusal to engage. It seems to harness all the lacklustre
energies of the early twenty-first century.

'Whatever' is an Americanism that has quickly permeated its
way into all Anglophone communities, an expression of boredom,
exhaustion, refusal and frustration about caring for others. We find

'whatever' funny precisely because we're so anxious about it. 'Whatever' is the key defence of the teenager against the parent, the powerful word that negates, albeit only temporarily, the power of authority, leaving its recipient spitting with rage. 'Whatever' is a word uttered by the actually powerless in the face of inevitable coercion.

'Whatever' speaks to us about *indifference*.

The wealthy and developed post-industrial West seems both to require and to despise the state of indifference, and its moral and psychological isotopes. On the one hand – let's get this into the open straightaway – we actually need mental states of indifference for our psychological wellbeing. Uninterrupted mental stimulation would result in madness. Becoming indifferent marks an ending to states of emotional upheaval, endings without which we could not survive. We emerge from the misery of loss pretty much whether we like it or not. We get over break-ups. We go on living after those we love have died. We cannot care about everything all of the time. This is not to devalue the pain of trauma and mourning, simply to remind us that indifference, when it means getting over things, is a natural part of our cognitive apparatus.

On the other hand, we simultaneously view *moral* indifference as utterly reprehensible. Coldness, sadism, apathy are all states with a moral vector, descriptions of a failure to engage with others – which nevertheless preserve the echo of a relationship. You are never just indifferent, but always indifferent *to* something…and therefore never really indifferent at all. It is the *knowingness* of sadism that horrifies us.

So we can immediately see that 'indifference' has a whole spectrum of meanings, dependent on whether it is directed inwards or outwards. While it is a perfectly natural psychological response, part of a mental processing kit when it evolves out of a response to our own personal losses and suffering, it becomes morally reprehensible when it is a response to the suffering of *others*. We live, however, in an era where the suffering of others is represented for us in a perpetual spectacle. We can access, and are constantly bombarded with, the icons of suffering: starving children, weeping mothers, the aftermath of natural and man-made disasters – suffering on a scale we can do little or nothing to reduce. What strikes me is the way in which *indifference is produced in us artificially*, a side-effect of our own helplessness in the face of ungovernable suffering. We switch off mentally from images of mass destruction, but have intense debates about the doings of C-list celebs. It is easier to care about things that we know aren't worth caring about, than to confront what we feel we cannot do anything to alter.

What we seem to be suffering from is a mutation of our natural capacity for indifference into an artificially produced *moral* indifference. The natural mode of indifference we all need, to cope with the ups and downs of our personal lives, is being pathologised into a neurotic, guilty indifference at the parade of unhappiness we cannot prevent. Our own emotional apparatus is being served back up to us, divested of any link with political agency. The mutation of indifference I am describing is a very serious depletion of our capacity to move from emotion to action, in the face of difficulty in the world.

Whatever is the English title of a recent French film, itself an adaptation from a novel: *Extension du domaine de la lutte*, by Michel Houellebecq, who has been France's most successful cultural export since existentialism and the *nouvelle vague*. In a way, for similar reasons: his brand of disaffection is a middle-aged version of recoil at society's *mauvaise foi*, and there is little more compelling than refusal and rebellion. But for Houellebecq there is no way out of the mire. We are compromised, sexually ruined creatures, whose only hope is a future of cloning, and the radical separation of sexual pleasure from procreation. For him, connections between people are simply impossible. They amount to a set of pre-programmed responses, riddled with boredom, cliché and self-interest. Even sex, the subject by which Houellebecq is famously most preoccupied, is largely a matter of repetitive and mechanical indifference. His novels are as controversial as they are funny, but they are also strangely lifeless and rambling. He has made a living out of repeating himself, yet the reading public continues to buy his work. Houellebecq epitomises why indifference is both seductive and elusive – and dangerous. Houellebecq is a critic but also a victim of the problem he describes.

Houellebecq's targets are the May '68 generation, whom he accuses of selling out. In that sense he is a national writer, preoccupied with France. But his subject matter, sex and its mercantilisation, is ubiquitous in the wealthy West. In writing about the sex industry in Thailand, in his novel *Platforme* (2001), he further implies that nowhere is safe from the relentless advance of commodification. In the same novel he also proposes a link between the sex industry and terrorism. The topics he picks make him a global writer.

France's position as a global power, however, is under serious threat. The world is becoming more and more indifferent to what the French have to say. France has been at the heart of Europe, engaged in the most profound of the social and political revolutions that have turned Europe into its current form. But since, perhaps, May 1968, or since, perhaps, the fall of the Berlin Wall, and the dissolution of the Soviet regime, France has come to seem more and more internally troubled and lost. Perry Anderson has recently described this demoralisation in two brilliant review essays as a *dégringolade*.[1]

France is a good testbed for an analysis of indifference precisely because of its status as a well-established democracy, with a revolutionary past based on the highest ideals and principles, but a recent exposure to unemployment, immigration and social disenfranchisement, what is known as *la fracture sociale*. It is this mixture of idealism with frustration that produces the *morosité* of the French, and the literary and filmic responses that interest me here. The provocative indifference that is stitched into such cultural stereotypes as the Gallic shrug, and the longstanding French attitude of *je m'en foutisme*, is coming under severe pressure from the problems of multiculturalism, and the painful transition into the knowledge economy. No longer an *exception culturelle*, the French cannot afford to care less. Nothing suggests this more painfully than the November 2005 *banlieue* rioting across the country.

In an era in which revolutionary responses to political, economic and social injustice have come to seem merely a directionless venting of frustration, certain French filmmakers have been offering a parallel strategy of intimate attention. It is this strategy which seems to me to go some way to exposing the homogenising effects of political indifference. In the earliest meanings of the term, imported from the Latin, via old French into English, indifference was understood in a philosophical and moral sense to mean *impartiality*, a state in which one is not moved one way or the other.[2] Very quietly, it is French *cinéastes* who are restoring the full force of this lost meaning: they are turning the properties of indifference against indifference itself. Contemporary French cinema has turned to documentary narrative realism: a patient observation of the local and the particular, the marginal and the disenfranchised. They exploit the properties of documentary for suggesting neutral observation, in order to show us that nothing is ever wholly a matter of indifference.

The roots of this fascination with narratives of quiet despair extend back further than the end of the twentieth century. Alain Resnais is a particularly important reference here, with post-war films such as *Nuit et brouillard* (1955) a major example of how documentary works to release affect in the viewer, and opens out local, individual incidents to a universal significance, without indulging in sensational imagery. Resnais's film sets out to discuss the Holocaust, but without showing any graphic images of suffering. Instead, we are shown the empty camps, and a voiceover by Jean Cayrol narrates what took place in them. The bleak understatement and the absence of drama – the disjunction between what we see and what we hear – functions like a screen onto which the viewer projects thoughts and feelings. Rather than supply provocative images, which undoubtedly feed, but also flood, the viewer's ability to react, Resnais practises a hovering, suspended withdrawal from his subject matter which enables us to explore sorrow, guilt and shame.

Agnès Varda is another key link in this history of intimate attention, although it is not until she begins to make films such as *Sans toit ni loi* (1985), and later *Les Glaneurs et la glaneuse* (2000), that her compassionate yet detached focus reaches its fullest development. Varda focuses on life's gleaners, the poor and disenfranchised struggling on the margins in *la France profonde*. She brings them centre stage, listening to their stories, without judging them or reorienting them inside a ready-made political argument. It is because there is so little framework to *Les Glaneurs* that it leaves us with such strong feelings of compassion.

Varda's films, however, are not easy to watch. The vagabond girl in *Sans toit ni loi* is unpleasant, foul-mouthed, exploitative, no romanticised Cinderella. Varda's camerawork breaks through the glaze of compassion and its complacent self-interest, challenging us to keep watching the impoverished lives on display. As viewers, we are gleaners too, although only ever temporarily. There is always an uneasy tension between what might be recuperated as a celebration of marginality, and the kind of compassion which ignores the object of pity altogether. It is this tension which animates Varda's work.

Mathieu Kassovitz's explosive *La Haine* (1995) relaunched the focus on the marginal. His portrayal of disaffected Parisian suburbs through the eyes of three friends – one *beur* (second-generation French Arab), one Jewish and one Black – caused a sensation. It reached even the French government. Kassovitz spliced the potential of film as polemic with film as entertainment. A thumping soundtrack, dramatic black-and-white film stock, and fabulous camerawork, accompanied a tale of police brutality, petty crime and aimlessness. Yet his aggressive style actually works to preserve the problems of the Parisian *banlieue* in aspic. It is a matter of inevitability that at least one of his three young heroes will be killed. The bitterness of his tragic plot leaves very little room for redemption, optimism or political agency. There is a sense of righteousness about this melodramatic realism, which, while it seeks to provoke change, also refuses to countenance the possibility of change.

So it is directors such as Claire Denis, Erick Zonca, Cédric Klapisch, Nicolas Philibert, Laurent Cantet and Robert Guédiguian who interest me more. There are very few guns or rocking soundtracks in their films. Instead they seem to track alongside their drifting, makeshift subjects.

I want here to focus on the work of Cantet and Guédiguian, both of whom are fascinated by the effect of social indifference on the individual. They both privilege story over fact, while using a documentary style of sustained attention and realism. There are elements of soap opera, or melodrama, and even the horror genre, mingled into their documentary film techniques. The meat of their tales comes from the examination of relationships broken or breaking down, under conditions of social and economic duress.

Their films act out the argument that community is corroded and compromised through the encouragement of an individualism based on the acquisition of material possessions. But they do not assert this. The effects of indifference, in their films, emerge as the unravelling of connections between people.

Guédiguian films people out of work, or clinging to low-paid, low-status jobs. Cantet films those struggling to play a credible role in the workplace. Guédiguian portrays the French underclass, while Cantet examines the tension between the working class and white-collar workers. Both choose small-scale subjects, and film in close-up. Most significantly, both explore the properties of the long take – what we might call a cinematographic correlate to the indifferent gaze – but they do so to very different ends.

Guédiguian, the son of a dockworker, has been making films for many years in his native Marseilles, in the working-class *Estaque* quarter, usually using the same actors. His leading lady, Ariane Ascaride, is also his wife. He is often compared to Mike Leigh and Ken Loach, as a filmmaker with an overt socialist agenda, but one fascinated by narrative as much as by politics. His latest film marks a departure from the Marseilles films, an adaptation of a book about Mitterand, *Le Promeneur du Champ de Mars*.

Guédiguian is best known for *Marius et Jeannette* (1997), *La Ville est tranquille* (2000), and *Mon Père est ingénieur* (2004). Of the three *La Ville est tranquille* is the hardest-hitting. *Marius et Jeannette* is softened by a love story, and goes the furthest towards romanticising the politically disenfranchised poor of Marseilles. *Mon Père est ingénieur*, on the other hand, offers the tale of a woman in a state of *sidération psychique*, a sort of waking coma. A community paediatrician, she suffers such a radical loss of hope about her work that she is paralysed by it. Her path towards this state is interwoven with fantasised reconstructions of her beloved Nativity scene, which remove the film from documentary realism, and blur genre boundaries. It is a deeply uncomfortable film to watch. The fantasised Nativity scenes come across as hopelessly idealistic and naïve, and it is impossible to know whether they are intended to be seen entirely as the perspective of the paediatrician, or whether they are also Guédiguian's challenge to our cynicism.

La Ville est tranquille is an angrier film, which occupies a middle ground between these two. It combines the portmanteau linked narratives of *Marius et Jeannette* with the dramatic loss of hope that characterises *Mon Père est ingénieur*. The film opens with a 360 degree panning shot of Marseilles, a smooth circular sweep, which suggests that the city is *tranquille*, but also teeming with life just under the surface. The narrative of the film echoes this diversity-in-continuity, with its structure of interwoven narratives. This preserves the twin pillars of randomness and coincidence, which condition urban life and the postmodern state. The film focuses most attention on Michèle, desperately trying to support a heroin-addicted daughter, an unemployed husband, and her daughter's baby.

Michèle, working in the fish markets, is clinging to one filament of the social net. The rest of her family has fallen through it, into unemployment and drug addiction. Indifferent she is not, yet she is the victim of a generalised social and political indifference to the plight of the poor and poorly housed, which, it is implied, has already claimed those she loves. It seems a matter of time before she too is engulfed.

The film works on a series of connections and repetitions. At one point, for example, we see Michèle take her daughter out to lunch in a shopping centre, trying to interest her in mainstream social activities, however banal. They have just left a scene of abjection in their housing complex apartment: Michèle's daughter prostituting herself for drug money. In the *brasserie*, they are served by a young black man. We already recognise him from his affair with a white bourgeois woman we have encountered earlier. This same boy will later be killed by a National Front supporter, during a random act of violence in the company of Michèle's good-for-nothing husband.

Michèle herself turns to prostitution, in an effort to save her daughter by buying the heroin herself. She is twice rescued by a taxi-driver. But then his benevolence turns to barter, as he turns up at her flat to cash in his chivalry for sex. Michèle numbly accedes. The taxi-driver begins to believe that he is conducting a relationship with her, despite paying her for sex. Michèle gets the heroin for her daughter from a childhood sweetheart, who runs a bar as a cover for his operations as a local hit man. The taxi-driver follows the hit man on one of his assignments, and they coincide at Michèle's flat. The comic rivalry between the ineffectual ex-docker, who has used his redundancy money to buy his taxi-driver's licence, and the hit man with his silent sexual presence, affords one of the few moments of levity in a relentlessly bleak film. But even this is destroyed when the hit man turns his gun on himself in the closing shot of the film.

This downward spiral of connections leads to a terrible climax. Michèle administers an overdose to her daughter. When we analyse the scene of the overdose, we can see a profound fusion between camera-work and subject matter that expresses one of the limit points of indifference: where the inability to filter out traumatic matter leads to a desperate act of self-preservation.

The scene breaks into two sections. The first is full of noise: shouting and tears. The daughter demands a fix over the crying of her own child, until her mother can take no more and gives in.

The second half of the scene is almost entirely silent. All emotion has been evacuated from it. Guédiguian uses close-ups and head shots at many points in the film, as a counterpoint to overhead shots of the city. The use of a long, still close-up is comparatively rare, but he exploits it ruthlessly during the overdose sequence. The camera hovers over Michèle's hands as she unwraps packet after packet of heroin, then moves to the daughter's face. We hear only the words 'Merci, Maman' over and over again.

Proximity and extended exposure to the subject form a direct visual correlate for the kind of indifference I am trying to analyse. They combine to force disgust as much as compassion. The viewer's mental apparatus for coping with personal suffering – the state of indifference – is artificially activated through the spectacle of another's distress. The viewer's response is an enforced and helpless identification with Michèle. We sit, as Michèle sits, watching her daughter die. The affective burden of the scene passes through the unwanted complicity of this identification: we watch the watcher. It is not the spectacle of the overdose that most turns the viewer off, since we do not see the injection itself. It is the bubbling sound of saliva at the corners of the girl's mouth as she thanks her mother.

Laurent Cantet is younger than Guédiguian, a rising star in French filmmaking. Although he also clearly has a socialist agenda, his emphasis is not so much on place as on *space*. *Ressources humaines* (1999) and *L'Emploi du temps* (2001) are both films that look at the workplace as a site of uncomfortable displacement. Guédiguian derives much of his aesthetic pleasure from filming a place he loves, and from firmly embedding his characters in a recognisable context, using bold colour schemes derived from traditional Provençal yellows and lavenders. Cantet, on the other hand, homes in on the codes that govern language use, organise hierarchies and social order, and structure behaviour in and around the workplace. Colour in his films is often secondary, subdued and flat.

For Cantet's middle-management or *cadre* protagonists, places, especially workplaces, have become interchangeable. Their mastery is a matter of speaking fluent *managerese*. Both filmmakers are rueful about a lost socialist spirit in France, but while Guédiguian is seemingly determined to resist the euphemisms of modernisation – rationalisation, downsizing, restructuring, casualisation – Cantet seems fascinated by the impact of such changes on different generations of workers. What makes Cantet's films compelling is the fine line he treads between observing, and participating in, the world he depicts. His protagonists are everyman figures, ciphers by virtue of the demands placed on them by society, but continually wrong-footed by their own pasts, their relationships to others, and their individual identities. He shows how the detached and generic language of the workplace is always a cover for more primitive and desperate emotions. He seeks the epic in the everyday.

Ressources humaines (1999) was Cantet's first *long métrage*, and tells the story of a rupture between father and son that also represents a reinforcement of class boundaries. The son, Franck, does well at high school and goes to business school in Paris. He comes back to do a placement, a *stage*, at his father's factory. He works with management while his father works on the factory floor. Franck comes up against the antagonism that exists between the unions and the management. He seeks a compromise, a questionnaire given to all the workers about the 35-hour week. Initially proud of his handiwork, Frank discovers that the questionnaire has been exploited to exclude the unions from negotiation. He further discovers that the management are about to use the questionnaire as a tool to lay off people, including his father, just before their retirement. At first believing in modern management practice, the son comes to side with the workers and organises a strike. There are echoes here of Zola's *Germinal*, and we anticipate something like the terrible showdown of the miners confronting the bosses. Instead, Cantet homes in on the tension between father and son. Franck's father refuses to participate in the strike, stupidly loyal to the factory, and there is a showdown on the factory floor between the two of them, witnessed by the other workers.

The rupture Cantet wants to show is not, or not straightforwardly, the son's rejection of his father's belief system. It is the damage caused by peeling back the protective layer of apparent indifference, which allows tension to coexist with everyday life. Caught between the desire to prove himself in the world, and the desire to prove his love for his father, caught between success and succession, Franck violently destroys both.

Cinematographically, Cantet does not use *cuts* to offer an analogue for rupture, breakdown, and fragmentation during this fraught confrontation between father and son. Instead he exploits, like Guédiguian, the cinematic properties of the long take, but for a completely different purpose. For Guédiguian, the long take affords an opportunity to challenge the viewer, creating an involuntary, unpleasant complicity between spectator and subject. In Cantet's hands, the long take is a visual analogue for the kind of indifference that wraps a protective film around potential rupture. Like Guédiguian's circular panning shot of Marseilles at the start of *La Ville est tranquille*, Cantet's long takes neutrally observe a microcosm of trouble barely masked by a smooth transparent veneer.

In order to signal the violence of the wound Franck inflicts on his father, in naming the shame he feels as his son, Cantet undoes the shot/reverse shot protocol usually adopted when filming conversation. Conventionally, the camera perches on the shoulder of the listener, showing the talker's face, and then reverses for the response. During the confrontation between Franck and his father, however, the camera rests on the father as the son is talking. Cantet emphasises the passivity of the father, his inability to change his situation, but also demonstrates the violence of Franck's attack. As Franck names the emotion that has run underneath the whole film, what captivates our attention for long seconds is the trembling of his father's lower lip.

The language in the confrontation scene is Racinian, invoking rejection, sacrifice, contempt: the spectacle of a son denouncing the father who gave up everything for him. It is language from another world, and detonates inside the bland euphemism of the language used everywhere else in the film. The only possible outcome is the expulsion of the foreign element, Franck. At the end of the film we see him return to Paris. He has won the local fight, and the strike is a success, but he has lost the personal battle.

L'Emploi du temps (2001), Cantet's second film, was loosely based on the real life of Jean-Claude Romand, who lived a lie for eighteen years, pretending to have a successful career, while scamming money from friends and relatives in order to support his family. His story was written by Emmanuel Carrère as *L'Adversaire* (POL, 2000).

Cantet's protagonist, Vincent, is caught between the desire to escape the constraints of professional life, while still wanting social recognition, the comforts of a good income, and the love and respect of his wife. When he is made redundant, he begins to drift, while maintaining the fiction that he has a new job with a UN agency in Switzerland. Ironically, he has to work hard to sustain his drifting life. He starts to swindle money out of friends and family, and later becomes a counterfeiter, in the company of Jean-Michel, brilliantly played by the real-life ex-con Serge Livrozet, who, having served time for social security fraud, now militates for prison reform. In a wonderful domestic dinner scene, Jean-Michel explains to Vincent's eldest son that he works to apprehend counterfeiters. In the world of the swindle, appearance and reality rely on exactly the same knowledge.

Cantet often films through glass – of buildings, or car windows. We see Vincent consistently positioned outside, separated from workers or family by glass. Cantet also often shoots at night. Repeated use is made of the mobile phone as an instrument of deception: the viewer sees more than the caller, and the increased mobility afforded by the phone enables Vincent to practise his deception. The mobile is a symbol, a poor metaphor, of Vincent's illusory freedom.

Cantet skilfully deploys elements of the horror genre throughout the film. The domestic scene to which we see Vincent return towards the end of the film is indistinguishable on the surface from 'normal' domesticity. It begins with one of many shots of Vincent looking at his family through the windows of their house. He is filmed from behind, and in the darkness, turning him into the intruder about to break into the family's innocent light. Once inside, the repeated calling for Julien, Vincent's son, to come downstairs to dinner, is both utterly naturalistic, and builds a fearful tension, for Julien has seen through his father, and refuses to appear. Here too there is emphasis on the father-son relationship, the interplay between expectation and disappointment. Vincent's other two children seem to expect something to happen and stare at their father. His wife turns her back in the kitchen, exhausted and depressed. When he jokingly asks 'if they are all afraid of him, or something', they say nothing.

The ending of the film has come in for some criticism, but in fact harnesses the same fragile capacity of indifference to suture reality that characterised *Ressources humaines*. Jean-Claude Romand eventually murdered his whole family when his lies were exposed. The outcome of Cantet's film is very different. All the tension of his dénouement lies in frustrating our expectations of a suicide or a murder. Vincent escapes from his own house as his father arrives to try to help him, drives away, and then leaves the car at the edge of the road to walk off into the darkness. The soundtrack of cars driving on a motorway suggests an anonymous death.

Rather than serve up the spectacle of terrible violence we expect as the logical outcome of the story, Cantet prefers to investigate the repression of violence – and the violence of repression – within the conventional social order. The abandoned car is not the final scene. His ending deliberately returns his protagonist to the bland and generic indifference of the workplace. Vincent's father secures him a fresh job interview and a second chance.

The final scene of the film is composed of a regular, alternating series of portrait shots of interviewer and interviewee. The regularity of the portrait shots emphasises the men's interchangeability, but also their disconnection from one another. Cantet seems to have shifted counterfeiting into the very fabric of the film. As Vincent is harnessed into role again, rehabilitated by the father, we experience confusion and a guilty disappointment. The disjunction between the viewer's knowledge of Vincent's recent past, and the bland euphemism he feeds the interviewer, opens an abyss. Complicity is established between the two men on screen, but refused to the viewer.

The false resolution, which simply shuts down Vincent's *dérive*, his drift, acts as an abstract jump cut in our expectations: how does Vincent come back? How is he reconciled with his family? And it emphasises Cantet's withdrawal from the private accommodations of his subjects. Once again, Cantet offers indifference as an impoverished means of salvation: the detachment of the workplace, and the compassionate withdrawal of the filmmaker. It is salvation evacuated of any spiritual or moral content: Vincent has been saved, but at the expense of his individual identity.

Guédiguian exploits the long take for dramatic purposes, alongside several other cinematic techniques, the overhead shot, the circular pan, and close-up head shots. Cantet, on the other hand, makes the long take his cinematic sentence. He operates visually in the horizontal plane, and rarely includes a scene without a human subject, unlike Guédiguian, who moves between the particular and the general, with his interlocking narratives and views of Marseilles. While Cantet shows how vital indifference is to stitching together our makeshift accommodations with reality, Guédiguian eschews this definition of compassion. His long takes are riveted to the despair they document. Guédiguian's mise en scène, the close-ups enforced by his claustrophobic interiors, reproduces in the viewer the exhaustion we see in his central character. Cantet relies on a visual litotes, an understatement that invites us to examine the constructedness of our social roles. But he refuses to rip them to pieces in the drama of his films. Guédiguian, on the other hand, forces us to assume the responsibility for his characters' tragedy.

The work of Cantet and Guédiguian suggests that it is possible to restore one of the lost meanings of indifference – that is, its sense of *impartiality*. It is clear that Cantet gets closer to this ideal – Guédiguian is warts and all despair. Cantet offers us partial, deliberately unfinished statements, and depictions of the cruelty of modern working practices. Guédiguian shows us things falling apart. Cantet shows us things cobbled together. Guédiguian rejects indifference as wholly bad. Cantet sees it as provisionally necessary.

Cantet is the more fashionable filmmaker. His visual under-statement is easier on the eye than Guédiguian's uncomfortable scenes of deprivation and despair. Yet even as we celebrate the possibilities of the indifferent camera eye, perhaps we should ask ourselves whether the neutrality Cantet is so tolerant of might not blank out his very efforts. The calm focus on the particular that characterises the best filmmaking coming out of France at the moment advocates political change that would empower the disenfranchised, but itself runs the gauntlet of marginalisation. The very neutrality of Cantet's cool camera risks being subsumed by the dominant order, which seeks to suppress difference, and to silence those with already weakened voices. Exploiting the slippery and reversible properties of indifference in order to expose them always threatens to backfire.

---

[1] *London Review of Books* 25, no. 17, 2 September 2004.

[2] Looking at the OED, Lebaigue's *Dictionnaire Latin-Français*, the *Dictionnaire étymologique et historique du français*, Littré's *Dictionnaire de la langue française*, the *Trésor de la langue française: Dictionnaire de la langue du 19e et du 20e siècle*, and *Le Petit Robert* yields some fascinating definitions and contextualised uses.

Jennifer Maiden

George Jeffreys: Seven:
George Jeffreys Woke Up in New Orleans

George Jeffreys woke up in New Orleans.
George Bush Junior was on the TV, obsessed
as usual with Baghdad. The TV should not
have been working, thought Jeffreys, as the street
below flashed with powerlines in water.
    Hiss.   He looked at black
water already blacker with blood, shit and all
the opals of oil. The TV changed to a group of women
wailing in funereal harmony:
          'Kiss me mother, kiss your darlin'.
Lay my head upon your breast...I am weary,
let me rest...' George Jeffreys was weary and
so, anyway, had been New Orleans. Weary.
          He was searching
for Clare, his not-quite-girlfriend, who herself sought
some victim or other in a local prison. George had driven
in on the Highway next to the Mississipi, where
the levees were okay. The storm had started,
was now keening like a train around the building.
Another keening noise outside the window, George
saw was a thin black man clinging
upright to a lamppost. At first he had looked
as if testing how long he could stand in a storm –
but now, George thought, the guy could not let go
for fear of flying debris, powerlines. George felt that
Bourbon Street was probably undamaged and a bar

seemed more attractive than this, so he left
the room and the TV, ploughed over to the lamppost,
helped the man that much further down the road.
In a brothel's bar full of candelabras, George
and the black man drank Southern Comfort. On
the wall was a photo of Robert Johnson, the
guitarist-singer who was sometimes not mentioned
around here, being said to have traded
his soul to the Master of the Crossroads. Jeffreys's
impressions of Voodoo had usually been benign,
however, involving much dancing, trancing and
a gorgeous goddess Ezili, clad in blue. For such
a weary town, this was not a tired religion. A TV
in the corner blurted on, the same
group of singing women: 'I am standing by the river
Angels wait to take me home...'

        In the sixth hour of the storm,
George left the Southern Comfort with his friend,
forced open the door
and walked back towards the nightflood, easily
for the wind walked for him. Soon a broken angel
in stone floated past, and too distant a tiny
nightdress or a child. Waiting-weariness will lead
always, he thought to violence. As a child,
Clare had killed her younger siblings

              for no-reason

              for some reason

that seemed to have significance tonight.

          The water
was black salt. Ezili was a seawater spirit

from ancient Dahomey. He focused on
her and not the crossroads, the sighing black street,
                          but suddenly there was
Clare liquid with rain, in a blue dress
like Ezili with trance eyes, walking.
                    Jeffreys
touched her with both hands and the electricity
numbed him to his spine.She held a white, purring
kitten she had somehow pulled from some
electric wires, and George soon guessed
she had spoken with the Master of the Crossroads
of whom he no longer felt afraid. She said,
'If you do want to meet him, you should probably
do it now, before the flood.'
'The flood?', asked George, puzzling biblically, but she
added dryly, 'Just the levees – when the waters
"stabilise" tomorrow it means that this whole city
will have become part of Lake Pontchartrain.'
                So Jeffreys
followed her back down through deeper water
to a place near the Garden District. They could hear
the Mississippi singing like a choir. The Master
of the Crossroads leaned back smoking
a roll-your-own, his face thought George, that of
that photo in the bar of Robert Johnson,
looking slim and black and much-too-young,
in a hat.   Clare whispered,
'He's obsessed with George Bush, Junior. I told him
you'd met Bush, didn't mention that
you probably saved his life,' the last fact still

clearly made her bitter. George didn't fancy
a dark night analysing Bush but the Master
drowned his cigarette under neat shoe in floodwater with an odd
pink smell of jasmine and said, 'I will
tell you about the buses, Mr Jeffreys,
do you understand about the buses?'
George said, 'Yes.' But the Master continued,
'The buses don't come, but to Bush
the buses exist and are moving people
out in an orderly fashion. To him, they're as
real as his chain-of-command. Iraq, he thought,
was to prove him his chain-of-command. I know
how this man thinks, Mr Jeffreys. He experiences
nothing but an ideal, or the chaos of the real,
                    he can't combine
the two into a bus that transports people.'
                        George nodded: 'That
I find is the problem of evil.'   The Master
held another cigarette from somewhere, offered
it to Clare, who declined it,
with her lovely, polite blue eyes. He said,
'And you don't smoke either, do you, Mr Jeffreys?
                        Sorry
 I can't offer you any wine and my bourbon
is in storage for some time. So your impression
of the President is much the same as mine?'
                        Clare's expression
dared George to relent a second time, but he said,
'He doesn't have to face a new election.' Then the Master
said, 'There are more than two elections,' with a tone

of sentimental satisfaction, and was gone.

As they walked up, Clare said, 'You know I was quite

nervous to go there, after everything I've done.'

                                        For some reason,

George kept expecting

the cat to become a baby, but it sat

as still as a statue in her arms.

Jennifer Maiden has won the NSW Premier's Award for Poetry twice, the Victorian Premier's Award, and the Christopher Brennan award for a lifetime of achievement in poetry. Her latest collection, *Friendly Fire*, containing the first six 'George Jeffreys' poems, was published by Giramondo in 2005.

Hoa Pham

Yolk

A Short Episode

Hoa Pham is the author
of four books: *Vixen,
Quicksilver, 49 Ghosts*
and *No one like me.*
Her work can be
checked out at
www.hoapham.net.
'Yolk' was written with
the assistance of a grant
from the Literature
Board of the Australian
Council.

Narrative is a form of hindsight. A way of drawing patterns from random experiences. Making sense of life with crises and turning points – as if life itself can be granted closure.

The mind will always strive to make patterns and make sense of the world. Even in the most obscure ways.

My mind is playing at pick up sticks. Somehow I have to piece it all together and make the structure stable. Somehow sort out the lived experiences from the hallucinations. All of my perceptions are suspect, what is most vivid to me cannot be depended on to be the most true.

I am a lucky person. I have recovered, they say, quickly. But I can see what I have lost, the world is now flat, almost in monotone instead of glowing with auras of light. I go to work and hide what is wrong with me, I only work half days and no one notices when I go home.

My mind is in fragments so I tell the tale in fragments. In the green of the hospital the vividness has faded. I used to get jolts of half memory, recognise the nurses that would bring me food, that I ordered in secret, hiding from the mirror that was a window into my world. The patients look like people I know, a man I knew who worked for Echelon, an ex-boyfriend who glowers and intimidates women. But up close confirms the lie, the nurse would tell me that she is not who I think she is. One of the patients, my next-door neighbour who carries around a soft toy lobster and wears bandages on her wrists, tells me she is not supposed to speak to me.

There are occasionally people here that I do know. One of them, a former colleague, knocks on my door by accident.

'Hello Kim,' he says and I greet him with his name.

'I didn't see you here,' he says and goes to the next door.

Another patient comes from Odyssey House. Her caseworker knows me too.

'Is she here as a patient or as a worker?' she asks the substance user.

'I think she's a patient. She's all right.'

It's different being on the reverse side of the counter, on the inside of the intake system, watching others talk about you. I think the nurses treat me like a human being most of the time. They come in and check on you at night with torches and you cannot lock the doors. Just like being in a hotel – except for the checking on you part.

I'm not allowed to walk around the hospital by myself. It means I stay in my room sleeping most of the time until my visitors arrive. My room overlooks the garden between the hospital and the clinic offices. There's grass and occasionally I see people walking around, usually not by themselves.

I do not want to see my parents. I remember that to discipline me and my brother they used to lock us in a cupboard. My father would make my mother lock us in then he would let us out.

I've been sorting through my memories. Trying to order them out from the hallucinations. I can do this now I'm not so tired. Before I was asleep most of the time. Now I'm not and I walk that line between being fully conscious and just drifting, drifting away.

Grandmother

My grandmother saw cats meowing at the back door, lots of them.

She was living with us and shared a room with me when I was younger. I would wake up at night and hear her muttering to herself in Vietnamese about the cats. They were scratching at the windows and the doors waking her up.

There was only one cat, Polyphony – Polly for short.

Polly slept inside and only meowed in the morning for her breakfast.

I stayed home and took care of my grandmother one day a week so Dad could go to work.

By then she was on medication and had calmed down a bit.

She showed me her rashes and told me about the cats.

What little Vietnamese I knew helped me decipher that she was talking about cats that weren't there. Three colored cats like she used to have in Vietnam that would yowl for rice every day.

My grandmother would scratch herself bloody and make her rashes worse.

Grandma had survived the chaos and the Vietnam war. She didn't have flashbacks to the war – she flashbacked to the cats. She talked to Grandpa too. Grandpa who was deceased a few years ago.

My brother and I decided that talking to Grandpa was all right. They had nine sons together and were by each other's side every day for decades.

When she talked about Grandpa she was fine. It was the cats that bothered her, the cats, the cats. She would get agitated and scratch again, like the cats would scratch at the door.

Mother

My mother was from Saigon – so she would say. The truth was her family spent most of the time on the run. Her father was a teacher and also a Nationalist. The family had to change their name and move to Saigon.

Mother never talked extensively about what she experienced growing up in Vietnam. We'd get little anecdotes at odd times, whilst sitting at dinner she would reminisce about how much she enjoyed living on a farm where the children would do some of the chores and look after the ducks.

Mother did not like talking about the war. Once when we were shopping she told people she was Fijian, or from the Philippines so she wouldn't have to talk about the war.

Once she was caught out and was very embarrassed. She could not speak Filipino back.

My mother and some of her sisters are very anxious people to be around. Mother once told of a time when her eldest sister would cling to a pot of rice and protect it.

It's mine – she would say. All mine.

Mum and Dad never experienced a refugee camp. They were lucky enough to be in Australia and naturalised. The family reunion scheme enabled my father to bring most of his family over to Australia. My mother's family divided and fled to Australia, Germany and the United States.

Mother said that teachers were viewed with suspicion and were spied on in Vietnam. They would be asleep and suddenly wake up and see the head of a person move at the window. The spy would duck once he was spotted. Her father had been imprisoned once already.

So I already come from a paranoid background – at least from Mum's side.

What is more likely – that my mother was taught how to strip and load machine guns at school – for a show of strength – or that my father – who does work in the public service, spies for ASIO?

What happened?
I was hit on the back of the head with a hammer.
Why a hammer? Why not a large object?

I was hit on the back of the head with a brick.

How do you know when you were hit from behind?

Because I saw it coming out of the corner of my...

Yes. You see. We can't have you making wild statements to the police now.

Test

Banana, coffee, cherry.

One of the cognition tests wound its way into my memory. I was programmed by a hypnotist counsellor to remember bits at a time. Each bit would be prompted by a change in the objects he would ask me to remember.

Banana, orange, cherry.

Merri Creek.

Merri Creek runs through the back ways of a chain of suburbs into the Yarra. It winds past an old convent, an environmental park, a school oval and a concrete structure which is used by kids as a skateboard ramp. Alex and I would walk by Merri Creek, where a series of attacks had occurred.

Banana, orange, cheese.

One of my friends had been harassed and stalked. I couldn't do much for her except tell her to go to the police. Then I saw a picture of the stalker in the local newspaper. He was a local artist and being lauded for his work. It made me sick.

Chocolate, orange, cheese.

I had talked to Alex about this friend while walking along Merri Creek. I cried and he held me in his arms. We fell asleep companionably next to the creek on a sloping bank.

Chocolate, lemon, coffee.

The local artist overheard us around the bend of the creek. He came by and pushed Alex into the river and I couldn't stop him.

Bread, lettuce, vegemite.

I am getting so confused, even my therapy is rewriting itself.

Hospital

In the hospital I look through the window out into the garden between the hospital and the outpatient clinics. I see birds, sparrows and Indian mynahs perched on the trees.

In my imagination, and I am sure it is my imagination this time, every person has a bird like a shadow familiar. Business men have pigeons, with their minor variations, purple necks or a flash of a green underwing. Other people have sparrows, that fly in flocks, wheeling in the sky.

I keep thinking I see people I know in the hospital.

Every day I take my lilly-pilly pills and the small round tablets that calm me down.

My friends come and visit me. One of them tries out the security, shows them her student card, wanting to observe the training tapes of me that they have been doing for students.

She really is a psychology student, and she is horrified when they do show her an observation tape.

At least that is what I think she says when she visits me.

Later, looking into the mirror, which I thought was a camera, I realise that this would be impossible. They would have needed me to sign a consent form and I never did.

My mind is like a deck of cards. I keep shuffling, and play mental solitaire, trying to fit my memories together and find all the links, to place them in the right order.

Echelon

Once I had kissed a man I knew had worked for Echelon, the information data gathering agency, in New Zealand. He was in Australia studying a masters in computer security. He told stories like how the security wing was obvious because there was a building with six floors and the lift only went to level 5. On level 6 you were asked embarrassing questions about your personal life. One of his referees had told them that he slept with a lot of women, and he said at the time it was true. And he was embarrassed that it would be on his security record for the rest of his life.

He did not sleep with me. We only kissed, I went home and a few days later he indicated he didn't want much more than that. He was also banned from travelling to some countries and that included Vietnam.

In Canberra the urban myth is that under the steel eagle monument in front of the defence complex is an American bunker.

In Vietnam writers and teachers are watched. Writers have their work banned, and are exiled, like Pham Thi Hoai.

In Australia I think things are different.

But it is not out of the realm of possibility that they aren't.

Hospital

I look in my notebook and know that I have been in hospital for a few days.

    This morning I packed again and waited to be taken home.

    This never happens. I had to unpack and remind myself that I have to be here for two weeks. Unless I can show them that I can be trusted on my own. That when I see my friends and Alex I can stay awake. That I do not hear their voices speaking for them about fantasies that could be true.

One of my friends is involved in a group called The Forum. They have to complete a group activity that involves six people to change something. When he visits me he is buzzed by someone on his mobile.

— No I'm coming later, he says. This is too serious. Change of plans.

I never have the courage to ask him whether he and my other friend wanted to break me out of hospital.

Alex is my boyfriend. He has hypnotised me into thinking that he is my boyfriend.

Alex is my boyfriend. The real Alex comes and visits me after work every night.

He's a beautiful boy with long blond hair and wren-sharp blue eyes.

Alex comes and visits and so does Miriam, another friend. She looks at me and says — You have never had a hallucination in your life.

When Alex comes in she asks him whether I hallucinate. Alex says yes. He sat with me through it all, the worst of it all.

When I thought I was an ASIO plant.

ASIO

I thought that my mother and father were subject to sensory deprivation and taught a whole lot of refugee children how to survive immersed in a sensory deprivation tank. The children were from all over the world, from refugee camps. They were taught to go 'nova' when the time came to escape, like the Orson Scott Card novel *Ender's Game*, where in zero gravity the kids would gather in the middle of the battle room and then explode in all directions, bouncing off the walls.

I thought I could read Thai, Indonesian and Chinese. When my father gave me DVDs I told Alex that if they were in Chinese or in Thai the pirated copies meant that we were being bugged by ASIO.

I thought my father worked for ASIO as an agent, and I was a plant. That was what I told the duty registrar when Alex took me to the hospital. That there wasn't anything wrong with me and I was really an ASIO plant.

No wonder they admitted me. And if I hadn't agreed and signed the admission forms they would have certified me.

Gummi bear

My consciousness is like a gummi bear. It stretches and is transculent. In its own way sweet and beautiful. It's also melted at the moment.

I cannot stay active for more than a few hours. Somehow the hours fly by in the hospital, I'm told that the drugs make me like a zombie, my afternoon naps are longer than I'd ever had before.

Alex is my contact with the outside world.

He first thought something might be wrong when I tried to entice the cat out from under the bed using jelly beans. I got one of each color and put them in order of the chakras. First red, then orange, yellow, blue, purple then white.

The cat did not come out.

My parents have come and given me candy. They visit every day and take me out of the hospital. I cannot be unaccompanied. And the girl with the bandages on her wrists told me she was not allowed to talk to me.

If she had I might have thought that she was someone that I knew.

Hello kitty

The Hello Kittys are watching me again. So cute with little bows in their ears they must be up to something as Alex would say.

I put them in the lounge room, to remind me we were being bugged.

When I went into hospital Alex brought me a Hello Kitty. I put her opposite the door watching with black beady eyes just in case something came in.

I knew I was getting better when I was able to put the Hello Kitty away.

I lose track of how much I tell Alex. I hallucinate that I am Lucy Liu's stunt double, that my brother and his boyfriend work for ASIO and trained at Oxford, that I'm really not myself but another younger girl. We pass on secrets that way, since all us Asians look the same, and we memorise names to know where we are up to, to spread the word.

In Vietnam plays are used to spread ideas, they are embedded in myths and opera.

At least with the most recent hallucinations now I am in hospital, slowed down by Zyprexa, I can see that they are hallucinations. I was never any of those things.

Yolk
I leave the hospital two weeks later. While in there I never learn not to eat too many eggs, one night I fart a lot and almost drive a visitor away.

I still need to sleep a lot and do not return to work for another week. Occassionally I hear something – like loud music coming out of the student household, saying that I set it off – I set off a trap. But I know to ignore it.

My sanity is like a yolk. It gels together despite the buffeting, but it only takes one sharp prick for it to leak into the white.

My psychiatrist says that a psychotic episode can happen to anybody – in my case out of the blue. I need to stay on medication to ensure it doesn't happen again.

Alex asks me to break up the line of Hello Kittys in the bathroom.

They remind him too much of what has happened. He remembers lots of things, including that I didn't like sleeping in red sheets – I thought that I was drowning in blood.

You have to appear normal, one of my counsellors said, the one I thought had put a hypnotic block on me. It was confirmed for me that I had never seen him before about being hit on the head with a hammer. So that was not true either.

Alex is alive, my parents are academics not ASIO agents.

I did not threaten anybody, or harm anyone.

Only Alex whom I occasionally mistook for the local artist, coming to get me.

I told the hospital shrink that he had hypnotised me into thinking that he was my boyfriend. But the shrink had already identified him, and knew that I was in the grip of psychosis – that I would see a threat in everything – even the person I loved and trusted the most.

I hit the back of my head on my desk at home. That's why I thought I had been hit on the back of the head with a hammer. I had read about it in the newspaper and thought it had happened to me.

The hallucinations gradually bleed away from me like paint from the landscape. The world bleaches out to shades of grey without the vivid reliving of my hallucinations. I do not remember much of the first week of hospital, I can only remember Alex coming to visit, and my mother coming in too.

– Can we go home now?
    – No. You're not going home today. I'll help you pack your things back in the cupboard again.
    – Why do I keep doing this? I wake up every morning knowing I'm going to go home and then I don't go home.

Silence.

Mother does not have answers for everything. I learnt this when I was a little girl.

Now I am learning it again.

In the second week I begin to live in time again. I look at my watch and am able to predict that mother will come in the morning, Alex in the evening. In between times I sleep a lot. Sometimes I walk around the hospital ward. Initially I wasn't allowed to go out of my room without someone accompanying me.

I begin to be able to look back and forth in time, in memories. Alex offers to be my guide – I can ask him whether something has happened or not.

I wince in embarrassment at some of my recollections.

– Do you remember when you said we were terminators?

I do. Alex and I were terminators made by my father. Every terminator was paired up with a terminator from a different race or cultural background. The terminators were not set to kill just yet. We'd go through a series of exercises that would rebuild our bodies and show that we were terminators. Every time something horrible would happen in the world we would go up a level. At the moment the terminators were locked in the heart. There was only two more levels to go before we would start hunting down and killing.

And when we locked down to go to sleep, it would be in an embrace, male and female terminator together.

I find that when I'm given instructions sometimes it is as if a vital hook or door in my mind is missing. I'm told something then I promptly do what I'm told not to do, and I cannot catch myself. I am told I'm in the high demand ward and I should not wander around the hospital – but sometimes I cannot help it.

Recognition

I suspect that psychosis is pattern recognition gone wrong. Everytime

I see someone who resembles someone in my memory I immediately think that it is them. I look back at what I thought about ASIO and Echelon, and think that my psychosis was making patterns from what could exist.

I think that the woman who brings in my breakfast is a Vietnamese girl who adores my work – who somehow recognises me and sneaks into the hospital.

One of the other patients is definitely from Echelon and so is his best mate – his brother.

The predatory male in the ward looks like my ex-boyfriend. He tries to paralyse me in the queue for medication by staring at the base of my spine. I move my energy consciously up my spine and turn around sideways so he cannot stare me down.

– What? Usually women freeze when I do that.

– She could freeze you if she wanted to.

Another patient joins in.

You know that something is a hallucination if it has a threatening aspect – the psychiatrist tells me as he drops by on the fly. I don't tell him everything that happens – if I did it would take too long. The nurses ask me questions too. I find it a strain to talk to strange people – I did even when I was not in hospital.

I suspect the staff expect me to remember instructions, they remind me when I say things that are out of line. I start writing again in an exercise book – of thoughts and feelings – what feelings I do have. I suspect if I wasn't so sedated I would be crying a lot.

I remember being held by Alex on the day of the anniversary of my grandfather's death, crying for all the dying people.

Alex berates himself for not realising I was sick. He should have realised. He didn't want to believe that I was that sick or even worse making it up for attention.

I told him to talk to someone else about it – to tell a friend – not to keep it to himself. He offered to tell me once which friend he confided in – and I said it was up to him. He still hasn't told me who – and I don't want to look at all his friends and wonder – is it you who knows?

Alex takes me home for the first time over the weekend. We go to our apartment and make love. It is the first time we have had such a long break between sessions. The warmth and immediacy brings me almost to myself again. Then I sleep in his arms for the rest of the time he is allowed to take me out of hospital.

Now I have a secure grasp of time. There is only three more days to go till I'll be allowed to go home. My immediate supervisor at work knows I'm in hospital. A card was sent from the team to wish me well.

I suspect I have schizophrenia. Although I know that you need to have two psychotic episodes within six months – otherwise it is just schizophreniform. These two words make such a difference. One is isolated – full recovery is possible and with enough medication will not reoccur. The other has the taint of movies – mad geniuses – the possibility of violence.

I have to hide my experiences from others, not flinch when they say they are going crazy, when they have not touched that schizoid world of seamless delusion that your mind can invent for you. I have not since had that certainty, the certainty of the delusion – it gave me a surety I never have in real life.

I do not miss it. The world has slowed down, has gone quiet.
     And I am now silent within it.

Andrew Taylor
Night by night

Strawberries ripen by the back door.
Rain patterns a pond's surface
and fills the fountain to overflowing.

The fish hid for two weeks, we assumed
an egret or kookaburra had removed them
the way a surgeon removes cancer.

Rain falls with vertical precision.
Someone appeared last night at the gate
to the park, appeared and was gone again.

No wind. They rise strawberry red
under the pond's surface
which dimples where their mouths touch air.

What did she want? If I wait beside the pond
in the rain till 3 a.m. will she come again
to the park gate? This geometry

of perpendicular rain is ruffled
by a rising breeze. Is it her passing
that is stirring the leaves? The surgeon

has finished his work and the body's labour begins.
Strawberries hang by the back door
and rain for a moment hides as the fish hid.

She will come again at 3, I know it
the way a shoulder presages rain.
3 a.m. By the gate leading to the dark park.

Andrew Taylor's *Collected Poems* was published by Salt Publishing, UK
in 2004 (www.saltpublishing.com).

Noel McKenna

Home Delivery

Born and raised in Brisbane, Noel McKenna has lived in Sydney since 1981. His work has been featured in many solo and group exhibitions, in Australian and internationally. In 2002 and 2005 he was the winner of the Wynne Watercolour Prize given by the Art Gallery of NSW. He exhibits regularly at Darren Knight Gallery in Sydney, Niagara Galleries in Melbourne and Greenaway Art Gallery in Adelaide.

I was probably around nineteen when I began to paint. I had dropped out of architecture at Queensland University in 1974, and one of the first images I remember doing was the view from the back steps of my parents' house in Brisbane, sitting and painting the backs of the two houses from the street next to ours, which was called Whynot Street. (A few years ago I sold a painting to someone who lives in a house on Whynot Street in Brisbane.)

Over thirty years later, I am still doing houses...

My life has been in the suburbs, so it is pretty hard for me to avoid houses as subjects.

A person's home does say something about the person; the colour it is painted, the style of architecture, garden design, fence. It all adds up to a vernacular portrait.

Many of the paintings featured here are of houses in the Sydney suburb of Merrylands. Merrylands was a suburb I had to go to and investigate, mainly because of its name. One of the first things I saw was 'The Happiness Inn', a Chinese restaurant which looked like it had been there for at least thirty years. It was an appropriate name for a restaurant in Merrylands.

Another reason I was drawn to this suburb was that I had read a newspaper story about residents who had built large devotional, religious structures there, and Holroyd Council were wanting to pull them down, as they had not submitted development applications for them.

I went on three quite long walks around Merrylands and found no religious structures which looked like the ones in the paper. But I was drawn to the older fibro houses in the suburb, which were of a pretty standard design, only differing from each other by colour, fence or garden design.

I began each walk at around 10 o'clock on a weekday, so there were not many people around, although one man, Tony, did come out of his lime green house to ask me what I was doing.

After I had I assured him that I was not a potential burglar, he told me how he'd bought his '50s house back to heritage condition. His attention to detail was praiseworthy. He had used about seven different shades of green.

I also had a large untethered pit bull terrier come charging at me, only to be saved by the dog's inability to clear the fence.

I work from photos and sometimes in the glare of the sunlight I don't know what I am shooting.

I went to Japan last year. After I returned, I developed a roll of film that had been in my camera and discovered a Merrylands house with a Japanese garden in the front.

I made a trip back to Merrylands to make sure it was there.

I couldn't help but be impressed by the kind of effort that people make to be different with their gardens.

Usually, when I travel somewhere for an exhibition, I will go and take photographs of the place itself, and more often than not, of its houses.

Over the last few years I have done paintings of houses in Queensland, Broken Hill, Sydney, and Wollongong, and taken photographs of houses in Adelaide, Melbourne and Sale in Gippsland. There are obvious differences between them all in terms of design.

My next houses will be from Adelaide and rural South Australia. I like the flatness of the landscape and the way the houses sit so close to the ground (as opposed to a Queensland house). On hot days they seem to be half-melted, disappearing into the ground.

Homes are at the same time shelters, enclosures, cages, stockpiles of memories, repositories of unwanted goods, somewhere to feel safe, something to show off (my home is bigger than yours), somewhere to plug into the power grid and run the television or to tap into the world via web sites.

When one is up in a plane, the overall view is of the sameness of suburbs and their houses, without much connection to each other other than the lines of communication for telephones and computers.

Despite this apparent blandness and similarity, when you look more closely you can pick out the details that differentiate them: the shape of the awnings, the colour of the guttering, the curtains in the front windows, all giving the houses a particular character.

Sometimes I am asked why there are no people in these paintings.

I reply 'because they are paintings of houses'.

Brick house, Burwood, 2005
oil on canvas, 60 x 70cm

Japanese garden, Merrylands, 2005
oil on canvas, 60 x 70cm

Catholic house, Burwood, 2005
oil on canvas, 60 x 70cm

Grotto, Burwood, 2005
oil on canvas, 60 x 70cm

Brown house, Merrylands, 2005
oil on canvas, 60 x 70cm

Green door, Merrylands, 2005
oil on canvas, 60 x 70cm

New branch, Burwood, 2005
oil on canvas, 60 x 70cm

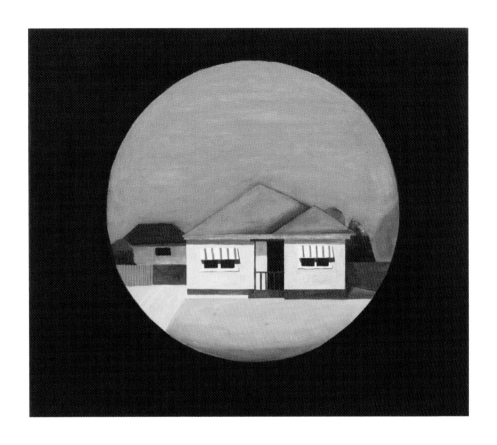

Light green house, Merrylands, 2005
oil on canvas, 60 x 70cm

Green house, Toongabbie, 2005
oil on canvas, 60 x 70cm

Home, Blue Mountains, 2004
enamel on canvas, 60 x 70cm

Ipswich house, 2004
enamel on canvas, 60 x 70cm

Turquoise home, Broken Hill, 2004
acrylic on canvas, 60 x 70cm

With thanks to:

Darren Knight Gallery
840 Elizabeth Street
Waterloo NSW 2017
tel: 02 9699 5353
www.darrenknightgallery.com

Greenaway Art Gallery
39 Rundle Street
Kent Town SA 5067
tel: 08 8362 6354
www.greenaway.com.au

Niagara Galleries
245 Punt Road
Richmond Victoria 3121
tel: 03 9429 3666
www.niagara-galleries.com.au

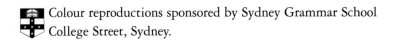 Colour reproductions sponsored by Sydney Grammar School
College Street, Sydney.

Emily Ballou

Creative Treason and the Power of Shame

Emily Ballou's first novel *Father Lands* was published in 2002. In 2003, she was one of the *Sydney Morning Herald*'s Best Young Novelists. She is currently working on a second novel set in the Snowy Mountains.

There are times in life when the question of knowing if one can think differently than one thinks, and perceive differently than one sees, is absolutely necessary if one is to go on looking and reflecting at all.
Michel Foucault

Re-imagining Black and White

There is an image I found while researching *Father Lands*, the novel I wrote about two families, one black and one white, coming together during an experiment in the racial desegregation of their city. When I say 'coming together', I mean I wanted to perform the work of integration, the work that didn't quite work the first time around, once upon a time in 1976, in a school in Milwaukee, Wisconsin. In the present-tense world of the book, it was the school that brought two children together, but in a bigger sense, it was also the entirety of American race relations, beginning, for my purposes, with Thomas Jefferson, that allowed the real intertwining of black and white to be re-imagined.

While researching the life of President Thomas Jefferson I found

an image of Monticello, the home Jefferson designed and his slaves built in the Virginia Hills over a period of forty years. It is considered one of the great historical American buildings, visited alongside the Liberty Bell, or the various D.C. monuments like the statue of Lincoln, and is featured on the back of the U.S. nickel (whose front Jefferson's face graces). In its time, Monticello was a Roman neoclassic architectural masterpiece. However, in this image I found, taken just after the Civil War, Jefferson is long gone, and too are those that purchased the place after his death, in bed, on the 4th of July 1826.

In this photo, Monticello has been abandoned. It is autumn, the dried leaves on the tree branches reach out across the picture; a picket fence has been erected in front of the building. I can't imagine a better metaphor for the incarnation (and incarceration) of the American Dream and its failure to provide for the average American citizen's psyche than a picket fence in front of Monticello, missing several teeth, peeling its Tom Sawyer whitewash, falling down. Monticello as squat: its windows barred up with wooden planks; newsprint pasted over the Civil War bullet holes in the window glass.

The photograph is in black-and-white, its pixels in my photocopy blown up, causing them to separate away from each other, further rendering its disintegration complete. Most Americans I'd hazard to guess, have never seen this photo of Monticello. It shows an underside of America that would embarrass or distress its more heroic, epic and mythological constructions. Today, Monticello's depression has been given a good dose of Prozac, its messy history cleaned up, all traces of its disgrace painted over in order to return it to its glorious Founding Father days of power. But the image of a less-than-perfect Monticello is part of America's history, part of its real struggle, its ongoing war with itself, and its doubt. It should be witnessed and spoken about as often as its polished, refurbished self.

I have always said that I couldn't have written *Father Lands* from within America. After moving to Australia when I was twenty-one, bits of my American brainwashing began to break apart, cracking open in the strangest places (while walking across the Harbour Bridge one night and being struck with the fact that I had no idea really WHAT Communism was). These cracks made room for previously Unthought Thoughts to appear, that I called my 'epiphanies of displacement'. The reading I give the photograph of Monticello is simply a testimony to one way I have come to re-imagine my country of origin.

But I see Australia as also like this alter image of Monticello. An act of hallucination that America brings into being, lets fall apart, makes disappear again. Australia's history is likewise familiar with the squat and with race relations' incarcerations. During the height of the response to September 11 and the War in Afghanistan, my father said to me, 'You must be very disappointed in America.' I answered, 'Well, Dad, John Howard's not helping anything himself, he's Bush's little lackey.' He said, 'Oh really? We don't hear anything about that over here.'

The dictionary defines squatter as: 'Somebody who occupies land illegally, especially somebody who takes over and lives in somebody else's empty house.' But the definition requires its second part, I believe, in order to really give resonance to us in Australia today: 'A person or animal that crouches down.' In order for somebody to take over the house, the house has to be empty, but if we were squatting down, as if to hide, if we were squatting down in some kind of shameful passivity, in false complicity to another country's agenda, then the house might appear to be empty when it is in fact not.

Are we letting our house appear empty?

If, as I see it, the writer's job is to be a traitor to his or her own nation, then what is the work of an Australian/American writer in the face of this hallucination? To love a country is to write about it if you are a writer. But to write about a country one must betray it in a sense too.

When I first fell in love with Australia I was blinded by Australia's perfect difference from America. I saw only its blue piercing skies, its Blue Mountain vistas, its sparkling Sydney floating on postcard water, its cleanliness, its lack of violence, and its vestiges of socialism. But fourteen years on, I have rubbed much blue paint off that sky; I can see the tarnish on the underside. If as a writer, I am looking at America as an outsider, I am therefore also looking at Australia as an outsider too, because the shame of white America gets relived here, reiterated every day.

Yet I stay because I have begun to feel that to run is to give up that work of examination, the re-imagining that came once I allowed the shell of my citizenship and my blind loyalty to a country to break open.

Creative Treason and the Power of Shame

The experience I had being bussed across town as part of the racial desegregation of the Milwaukee public school system was ultimately one of the most significant of my childhood, but it also brought to the fore or gave rise to certain kinds of shame that otherwise might have stayed buried. While at the time, I experienced these emotions as negative, as humiliation over my skin colour or guilt about the racial history of my country and my white ancestors, twenty-five years later, when I sat down to write my novel, I realised that those feelings of uncertainty – the simultaneous awe and fear I felt towards African Americans as a young child for instance – were ones that most people kept hidden. Yet by keeping them hidden we keep the wound festering. If our shame is ever to have a productive force, I believe we must speak up. For me, writing was one way to explore and admit to my own shame.

I wanted to write a book that gave voice to the incredibly important experience the Integration program was for me, as well as these unhealed, unspoken facets of shame and grief and ambiguity I still feel about race issues. Growing up in one of the United States' most segregated cities, I was taught that race 'was not an issue' in America. Just as some were taught not to question their hate, others were taught not to question their love and there was no room in either world view for ambiguity, for contradictory emotions, for doubt.

Coincidentally, I've ended up living in a country where there are many, many race issues and ambiguities and the Tampa crisis and the treatment of refugees in Australia were foremost in the news at the time I started writing the book and I think they triggered emotions from my childhood, things I hadn't reconciled yet. I realise now that this reliving of old shame during the process of writing and releasing the novel was just practice for the years to come. Over the last three years, there have been many more opportunities to revisit shame's irrepressible ache in response to John Howard's vision for Australia. There are many days when I sit in front of the television in a kind of paralysis of dejection, hopelessness and if I'm honest, passivity. All of these are forms of complicity.

Passivity *is* compliance.

Or maybe shame is what gets created in those of us more prone to depression and timidity, while those who are prone to anger and action find themselves more often in a state of outrage.

I'd like to explore the idea of shame vs. outrage a bit more comprehensively and see how each emotion creates a different energy; to explore whether shame and the regret it gives rise to can be used productively, as outrage long has been, as an agent for change.

Because ultimately, while shame is a deeply uncomfortable feeling, if it remains unaddressed, it only gets buried more deeply. It stays put like a lump of food the body can't quite digest. It oozes within. I think most people have learned to live with this lump in their bellies, to turn aside and avoid the heaviness it brings. Drusilla Modjeska suggests in *Timepieces* that the 'link between depression and un-examined conflicts can be true for a culture as well as for an individual', and sometimes I think of us, as a country, moving through our lives with an urban sandy cheerfulness or a laconic 'she'll be right' in order to mask over the heartburn of undigested sorrow, because it is simply too difficult, while managing the day-to-day aspects of living, to look up and really acknowledge what is happening around us.

Rather than avoiding these tricky emotions by looking the other way, we can confront them and find a way to use them. I am interested in how we might *apply* shame rather than outlining the *causes* of shame; how we might approach the issues more philosophically than prescriptively. For each of us, these causes will be different. For me, racism seems to trigger the greatest feelings of mortification and sorrow, but I am not a spokesperson for issues of race either here or in the United States of America. I speak only from my own emotional experiences.

While shame stays, quietly eating away, outrage comes and goes. Outrage must be heard; it flares up and dies quickly and then seeks a new target. Outrage's energy cannot be maintained continually over a long period of time. It has the fierce power of anger, indignation and violence. The riots in Redfern after the death of T.J. Hickey were the result of this kind of outrage. For all those that will chain themselves to doorways and take up residence in trees and take to the streets and throw rocks or kill themselves or others in the name of outrage, there are those whose humiliation and pain ticks away silently beneath the surface. In some people, un-addressed shame might be the cancer for which outrage becomes one chronic symptom.

How many of us watch TV in helplessness? As John Howard slowly and insidiously repaints this country in 1950s Frigidaire white? To my understanding, limited as it is, of life in the 1950s, and different as it was perhaps materially in America compared to here, what was the same, I sense, was a profound neurosis; a kind of overwhelming fear, that until September 11, seemed almost laughable in its small-mindedness and its paranoia. Once upon a time, they built picket fences to segregate and separate, defuse anxiety. Now they build barbed-wire fences, tape the windows with duct tape and pray for the same sense of safety. This fear is again being whispered, passed ear-to-ear and transformed utterly in the process, a rumor whose origins we don't even know, but perhaps, believe all the same. Such whispers can make fear real. This fear is explosive and dangerous; it has deadly consequences.

Who's to say that as a country, as a world, we are not quietly, progressively, determinedly feeding fear, causing hearts to pound, fueling the desire to run, to flee, to save ourselves first? Ninety-nine per cent of us would trample every other person that stood in our way if the fear was strong enough. What happened in New Orleans is a perfect example. Fierce and palpable outrage caused by fear, by desperation, perhaps by racism, poverty, sorrow and shame; whatever the reasons, it is real. It is not to be judged, but it is also the antithesis of peace, the antithesis of compassion, however natural it may be.

The shame we feel over the political actions of our present government is also real. It feels hopeless at times. We want to help. We might not know how we can help.

When I turn on the TV, I think to myself, what am I doing with my life? Sitting in a room and writing fiction? Is this in any way useful? But I have come to believe that writing, if it is harnessed in the service of bringing about greater consciousness or change, is an important act.

In *The Writing Life*, Annie Dillard writes that 'fiction cannot shed the world because its materials are necessarily bits of the world'. It isn't a question of simply transplanting the 'real' into the fantasy, but finding a way to let thoughts and threads that might never otherwise meet to be intertwined or juxtaposed – a sort of conceptual enjambment – in order to better illuminate our understanding of the here and now, and create what did not exist before. It is imaginative cultural history as a force for change. It is writing as an act of creative treason.

Treason is a provocative word in this day and age. But like shame, it is a word I feel in need of a revival. A reclaiming.

By its definition, treason is a violation or betrayal of one's allegiance to one's country. For those of us who are citizens of more than one country, as I am, there need not be a fear of divided loyalties when both of these countries seem to be of one mind. There is one country really: The United World of Fear.

A person is also seen to commit treason by aiding 'the enemy', but when the definition and location of 'the enemy' is forever shifting, how is a reasonably concerned citizen to know what might constitute an act of treason? If the 'enemy' is that which stands in hateful opposition to us; if 'the enemy' is that which is dangerous to our wellbeing, then it seems to me that for those of us who might feel our compassionate and true selves to be at odds with our 'country of allegiance'; who might feel that the fear being whispered to us daily is somehow dangerous to our wellbeing, not to mention many other beings' wellbeing, then it is also true that our 'country of allegiance' as we experience it day to day, might also be seen as 'the enemy'.

This might sound overly semantic, but semantics are the root of much of the fear we are fed. When words are slippery, used haphazardly, as if language had no real impact, or consequence, then their real meanings and their symbolic power are allowed to slide away. These words and their speakers are at times allowed to get away with murder. Literally. This is the state of language that Don Watson wryly calls a 'Death Sentence'. But as I have been suggesting, words are also an important part of the remedy, a cure for the undigested shame in the pit of the stomach, a cure for questionable allegiances, a remedy for fear. Words can be the question and the answer, the problem and its solution.

The writer's job, the artist's job is not just to write or paint or sculpt what you know best, as the saying goes, but to be a traitor to what you know best: to be a traitor to your country, to your own culture, perhaps even to your own sex. This means getting under the skin of things, pulling them apart, learning to *see* what you thought you already knew, differently.

When, after living in Australia for a few years, I began to have revelations about America, firstly, what it meant to be an American girl, then what it meant to be an American citizen, I began to see America in terms of its various brainwashings, its place in the world, its collective memory and founding stories, that unshakeable, Colgate-bright American Dream in an entirely new way. Understanding and then articulating this brainwashing was a form of treason. But creative treason can and should take many forms. It might or might not be an overtly political statement. It might also mean being a traitor to one's projected literary self, or to one's writing practices, by finding ways to produce and publish things that might not fit the current publishing climate.

Writing as an act of treason is a privilege one has only if one lives in a country that permits its artists to speak. If we are not permitted to speak on the other hand, writing as an act of treason becomes a call to arms. It is not just the control a government may exert over its artists and writers that we need to be afraid of, but also, when a livelihood is at stake, the control the publishers exert over what kinds of material find a home on the bookshelves. Or perhaps contentious material never even reaches the publishers and therefore, the public. Sadly, in a conservative publishing and political environment, we tend to be our own best censors.

What is it that we do not say; that we stop ourselves from writing?

I would not like to suggest that my own work is in any way exemplary or brave compared to the work of the political and sexual revolutionaries I admire. I am just as guilty of putting myself in a box, publishing the kind of writing that is expected of me and keeping quiet at times, because it is easier, about the things and parts of myself that shame me. But I do think the more we can play traitor to ourselves and our writing practices, even in small ways, the more interesting, truthful and daring our artistic community and country will be. When the truth about who we are is at stake, the phrase 'publish or perish' starts to take on a whole new meaning.

In the frightening political climate we now find ourselves, at a time where outrage is the understandably prevalent emotion in response to John Howard's sedition laws, the force that threatens to shut us down and shut us up, might equally become a force to pry us open again. We can use these new threats to our freedom of speech to really come alive again, both as a literary community and as writers. I feel a certain excitement bubbling in the air, because as soon as somebody says, 'Don't speak' the desire to speak is just that much stronger; the more I dare myself to say.

If treason is a question of allegiances, the way we play with our allegiances, then creative treason might be defined as an allegiance to the creative act in the search for larger emotional truths. It might be a way of using creativity to speak up against a country, or a self or a way of writing that no longer represents us, and, in doing so, release our most deeply buried shame.

For myself, writing *Father Lands* was one such act. Writing this essay is another. They might seem small, overly quiet acts, but who is to say what works and what doesn't when we are trying to change the world?

Maybe a writer's job is to come out quietly – from between the cracks. Maybe those that feel the most shame, have the power to fuel the most change. And while the problem with America is my problem because it is every thinking person's problem, it is also not my problem any longer.

Australia is my problem now.

Elizabeth Knox

A Hole in Our Maps

An Interview with Cristyn Davies

Elizabeth Knox is the author of seven novels, including *The Vintner's Luck*, which won the Deutz Medal for Fiction in the 1999 Montana New Zealand Book Awards, and the Tasmania Pacific Region Prize. In 2000 she was made a laureate of the Arts Foundation of New Zealand, and in 2002 an Officer of the New Zealand Order of Merit. Her latest book is *Dreamhunter*. Part Two of the Dreamhunter Duet, *Dreamquake*, will be published in May 2006.

Cristyn Davies is a doctoral student in the Department of English at the University of Sydney, and works as a research officer for the Narrative, Discourse and Pedagogy Research Group at the University of Western Sydney.

CD: I remember seeing a picture of you before we met. You were shot from below, peering out over what I imagine to be a scenic Wellington horizon. I love that image for many reasons; the gothic romance it evokes reminds me of Emily Brontë, a comparison that doesn't stop with the physical resemblance, but extends to your prose – particularly *The Vintner's Luck*. This black-and-white photograph does something more; it positions you as gazing into a landscape that I cannot see, and I am left to rely on you to animate this landscape, and other landscapes, real and imaginary. The landscapes in your novellas and novels are rich in detail, and are powerfully evocative. Can you talk more about this?

EK: That photograph! I think of it as my still-from-a-John Ford-film portrait, though I can see that it is rather gothic, too.

Actually, it is partly because of my love of film that I'm so concerned to build up a sense of whole real worlds in my books. Any film does this in a series of heavily textured instants – shots, that is. In a novel you have to use language. Not necessarily simply descriptive language. I think of my novels as consisting of scenes in which things happen, either the drama of an encounter between any number of characters or – a drama of a different order – the progress of a solitary character's experience of their thoughts, or feelings, or observations. Say – a realisation, a qualm, a rage, a want, a walk up a mountain path. My characters are inside their consciousness, consciousness made up of memory, of what's happening to them in the moment, and of expectation. They are inside their bodies. And they are in landscapes or in rooms. The whole, real-seeming worlds I want are made up of these characters' fluctuating attention to any of these things. So, for instance, in a scene in *Daylight*, Eve wanders around the town of Arles during a heatwave. The festival of the Arlesiennes is on and the town is full of Camargue horses and smells of fresh horseshit. The leaves on the plane trees are so dry they rattle. Eve creeps with other people along the shady side of streets. The stones reflect heat so she feels she is walking through warm air, and wading through hot to hip height. The freezers in shops have given up the ghost and the street is slicked by rivulets of fluorescent syrup from melted ices.

Well, that's what I remember writing. I just consulted the book and discovered it was a little different. To write it, both times, I'd consulted my own memory of being in Arles in a heatwave. The landscape in my memory is made up of smells and sounds and phenomena – the feeling of reflected heat, for instance. My landscapes are made that way, from memory, and from language – the 'street slicked by rivulets of fluorescent syrup' is phonetically oozy and melting. English has rhythms and tonal qualities that are, to me, often very evocative of phenomena.

Of course I invent landscapes too. Heaven and Hell in *Vintner*. The Place in *Dreamhunter*. In those cases I just use what I think of as imaginative insight. I think 'If this, then this'. Like – if there are no insects in Heaven then every leaf and blade of grass is whole and perfect and as symmetrical as possible. If all the illumination in Hell comes from the fires below then those fallen angels would lie around on the roofs of the palace, on their backs, with the books they are reading held above their faces.

CD: *The High Jump* – the VUP collection of your three novellas: *Pomare*, *Paremata*, and *Tawa* – has the subtitle: *A New Zealand Childhood*. What are your thoughts about the politics of location and the poetics of writing, and how have these thoughts shifted over the trajectory of your writing career?

EK: When I first decided to 'become a writer' (which is how I thought about it in my late teens) it occurred to me that, naturally, what I was hoping to become was a New Zealand writer. I knew New Zealand writers. I'd been in Sam Hunt's house at Bottle Creek – had a lesson from him, at twelve, in the distilling of vodka. Noel Hilliard was a friend of Dad's. For years Dad drove Noel to work and us to our college. New Zealand writing and history were often discussed during the ride. I first got drunk – on Ian Cross's cognac – with Noel's younger daughter Hinemoana. Denis Glover kissed my sister Mary at a PEN barbecue. So, when I began to write I knew quite a bit about the company I hoped to join.*

My first three novels, *After Z-Hour*, *Treasure*, and *Glamour and the Sea*, are all 'New Zealand novels' in the reductive sense of term, in that they are wholly or largely set in New Zealand. The novellas are, of course, autobiographical, as in love with their suburban Wellington settings as I have always been with the scenes of my childhood (even when terrible things took place in them). I do remember being vexed by one reviewer saying that they didn't really want to read anything set in a dreary Hutt Valley state house suburb, and another who said they thought it wrong of me to remind people of the time in which a wife would call her husband 'boss'. I was annoyed because I thought they were asking me to lie, to revise the past, to improve on it when it had been my project to tell what I knew – what only I knew – what had filled me with awe or fright or fancy, in my New Zealand childhood.

I've never had a plan about a territory in terms of location. I always assumed that, since I've lived all but six months of my life in New Zealand I was, by default, a New Zealand writer. Since *Vintner* though I have on a number of occasions been told that I'm not a New Zealand writer since I don't set my books in New Zealand (forgetting the three novels and three novellas that are set here, and that Southland in *Dreamhunter* is more New Zealand than not).

Anyway, what I wonder is whether it is setting that makes a book belong to a national literature, or sensibility? I think about the animator Hayao Miyazaki. His *Porco Rosso* seems to be set on the Riviera. *Howl's Moving Castle* seems to take place in the mountains near Alsace. And *Castle in the Sky* and *Kiki's Delivery Service* take place somewhere in Europe – maybe. But those films' islands, trains, mines, mountains, cobbled city streets are all part of the country of Hayao Miyazaki's imagination. His own place. And, somehow, his sensibility seems Japanese. And the Japanese sure know, and are glad, that they own him.

That's the good-tempered answer to what, for me, and not *because of me*, has become a bit of a vexed question.

This is the bad-tempered answer.

I could mutter on about our arts bureaucracy's obsessions with 'branding the national product', or about 'questions of regionalism' or 'an anti-romantic emphasis on the historical specificities of story'. Or I could talk about 'writing what you know' (I'm stuffed here, anyway, and even if I wrote books set entirely in New Zealand in the present day or recent past I'd not qualify since I'd still be writing fantasy). I could do all this, but I don't really want to let the public figure, the New Zealand writer, answer this question.

I think (I hope) that anything I can make my subject, I can make my subject. It's up to readers to judge how well each book manages this (hopefully readers with no ill-will). I'm just not the sort of artist who writes her books with a critic's finger held to her own pulse. There simply isn't time. So, I will confine my literary savvy to my reading, and to my interest in the production of effects in writing. I hope it isn't necessary for me to have to refresh my eyes with reference to my sex, my suburb, my country (or gender, class, nationality, since that's the talk). No – these are my eyes for only eighty years if I'm lucky, and so far everything through them still seems bewitching and strange. And I very much hope it isn't necessary for me to have to constantly replace myself with 'my times', as our cells are said to replace themselves every seven years – because time is long and life is short and I'm not the sort of cold, critical intelligence who needs to take seven careful years between each book.

CD: As a child growing up in Wellington, you played imaginary games with your sisters with whom you were close. And there we have another connection with the Brontës. How did these imaginary games become a sustained practice, and how do these games function, at the technical level of creating narrative, or telling a tale?

EK: I played with my sisters and friends. The initial game – or rather two games that became one – first existed between me, my sisters Mary and Sara, and my friend Carol between 1970 and 1979. I say two games because there was a long ongoing story we called 'The Saga' or simply 'The Game', and another I played at night with just my younger sister, Sara. 'The Saga' is the game I have talked about on and off, because it's marginally more respectable, and easier to explain.

In the night game Sara and I would take our characters and give them different lives and histories and tell a story about them over three to six nights. In my mid to late teens I kept a kind of diary of the stories where – for some reason now unfathomable to me – I wrote down the names our people had in each story and not much else. Perhaps I thought I'd remember the story if I remembered the names. (Actually I'm very happy to have those names – Valentine Laird, Roth Pendath, Astrid Brand, Tyrell Gray – this was the late seventies, early eighties.) I also wrote down scary statistics like, 'Of 131 nights, on 78 we played, on 53 we didn't.' We must have gone through our high school years chronically deprived of sleep. In fact I'm sure I remember Sara's history essays in the fifth form blotted with spots of drool where she'd put her head down for just a moment during class.

My diaries occasionally had other notes on what we were up to. On plot, or setting. For example: 'English public school 1920s. B. is a teacher they call the grey eminence. SF is a bullied pupil. C. is a lady parachutist.' We invented a romantic poet called Leon Barclay who disappeared – actually he ended up on Olympus with his god-admirers. Or 'X. is on trial for murder. Can he be saved if Y. clones his victim?'

Sara and I played at night, most nights, and on the weekend. Carol and Mary only spent weekends playing – much to the disgust of Carol's parents, who would rather she did gymnastics and swimming, and went off to the stock cars to work in their friend's hotdog stand. Carol gave up playing in 1978, when she got herself a boyfriend and resolved to grow up (rather like Susan in *Narnia*). Mary gave up when Carol did, because, she said, 'It was all too sad without Carol'.

That was true. Sara and I carried it on, but it was hard work, while our night game was as rewarding as ever. For when Carol quit, and dispersed her people into places on that world we never went to, her people's very best friends and family had to find reasons to fail to visit. Year after year, to fail to visit, until becoming estranged. It was horrible, and we were too young to know how lifelike it was.

Anyway, Mary came to her senses, or recovered from her grief, and resumed in 1982. Then – and this is when it gets really weird – in 1983 I started another game, by accident and as a joke, with Sara and her girlfriend Ailsa, and my friends Madeline and Phillip. That game – set in an imaginary, post-revolutionary South American country called Lequama – quickly became involved and serious. I introduced my favourite character from the other game into it (as a ghost). For months it seemed we were living simultaneously in a flat near the

Victoria University, and in the Presidential Palace in La Host. Then it was over. Ailsa departed when she and Sara split up. And Sara supposedly gave all such things up for good when she moved out of our flat (since we were no longer sharing a room that was the end of the night games too). Then Mary's small daughter Helen somehow made it impossible for her to carry on playing, and she stopped in 1985.

But, by that time, I'd managed to salvage and transplant what I could of The Saga. I introduced Madeline to the notion of the night game – of stories rather than saga. She had a pretty strong sense of her characters by then and took to the whole thing straight away.

The Saga/Lequama story became impossible to sustain the older we got. It simply took up too much time and seemed to require its players to live together – as siblings and later housemates do.

Madeline went off to study drama in Brisbane in 1994 – so all playing was suspended till Phillip, who had loved and missed Lequama, suggested he might like to try. For a few years I played games with Phillip. Then with Phillip and Madeline when she came home in 1998. (My own marriage and the birth and babyhood of my son never seemed to require the same sacrifices as the various lifestyle choices of my sisters and friends. My marriage was never to me a declaration that I meant to change my life and, when it came to motherhood, Fergus never thought of himself as 'babysitting' when he was in sole charge. I think I was lucky to have attached myself to a generous and *secure* man.)

Sara was living in Australia after '92, but always liked to play games when she visited. And then, last year, I discovered internet telephony. Sara and I can now lie in our separate darknesses, in Sydney and Wellington, telling stories, and staying up too late for people with busy lives (me two hours later than her!).

So, that's how it was sustained, with cunning and compromise and strange graftings of one thing onto another; with lettings-go and turnings-back. And it survived because I was there the whole time. I kept it going because I enjoyed it more than I enjoy most things, and because I found it was good for me, and useful to me as a writer.

At the moment it carries on between me and Madeline, and me and Sara. Phillip isn't doing it – but hasn't given up as such. He works shifts, lives forty kilometres away, and hasn't enough money right now for broadband.

How did the game work, technically? Well, we all had our own characters. My friend Carol had ten. Ten was what she could manage. I had hundreds, though they were never all onstage at the same time, but I didn't mind being responsible for the crowd in crowd scenes. We told our stories in the third person present tense. For example: 'He's cycling down the road when a car speeds past him, fails to take the corner, smashes through the barrier and sails off the bluff...'

It is a highly cooperative activity – but not necessarily polite. Players have to delight in surprising one another, and in being surprised. You can't want always to be the hero (Phillip had problems with this and was often having characters do things like produce white-phosphorous grenades at handy moments when it was by no means clear earlier that they were the sort of person to be carrying serious ordnance). Playing takes decorum, but isn't a decorous activity. If any player wants something to happen it has to unfold in a way that some-how charms the others into it – even if the charm is of an alarming nature. It isn't an activity that is commensurate with silence, or cool-ness, or carefulness, or sloth, or one-upmanship.

Its great, *great* charm has always been that of being someone else, somewhere else, and living a life more vivid and dramatic than one's own. (Or, in our teens at least, when we had a rampaging alcoholic father in the house, of living a life whose drama somehow *enforced* our sense of identity rather than assaulting and eroding it.)

CD: Recently I asked you which, out of the books you have written so far, is your favourite? You said that *Black Oxen* was the novel that reflected you most deeply, which interested me because I know it is the text that some of your critics found most difficult. How does your imaginary game figure in this novel, and can you talk more about why it is your favourite work so far?

EK: I should begin by saying something about critics. In New Zealand when we talk about 'critics' we are usually only talking about review-ers. A critic and a book reviewer are not the same thing. Here books are mostly processed by reviewers only. Of course I should also say that many *readers* found *Black Oxen* difficult. But by no means all. To some it was just what they were looking for. They're the people who come up to me after talks to whisper confidently that *Black Oxen* is 'the book of yours I really liked' and that they've read it 'twice' or 'several times' or even, proudly, 'six times' (a woman in her late sixties retired from running a corporation). What these readers respond to is part of what I like about it – its complexity, apparent digressions, its puzzle-like structure. This response isn't merely intellectual – the book isn't just a good workout for the brains of brainy people – it is also a book whose shape provides both the tests and proofs of the questions it asks about identity. It's a book in which several people, in order to work out who they are, apparently explore their own stories by telling them to others. In the framing narrative a woman tells her story (and her father's story) to a professional psychotherapist. But really she's telling the psychotherapist his own story. *Black Oxen* is a book with, ostensibly, three narrators – but really it has only two, and it's not till the very last sentence of the book that this becomes completely clear.

Another reason I like the book so much is to do with its shape. I mean, it's a book that explores the feeling many of us have, an un-decided, questioning, existential feeling about whether what happens to us is the result of accident, destiny or conspiracy. It's about those feelings, the hopelessness or happiness of recognising what happens as accident; our sense of wonder at the feeling we sometimes have of things being 'destined'; and how our sense of events being 'designed' sometimes suggests to us that there is some kind of conspiracy at work in our lives.

Because *Black Oxen* is the book that comes after *The Vintner's Luck*, a number of those reviewers, and at least one real critic, charac-terised it as a book written by a writer who has had some success and is now guilty of ambitious overreach. The fact is, it was the book I was always trying to write. My first, unpublished, novel, which I wrote when I was nineteen, was about my imaginary game – how I felt about it. I had another go at writing a similar book when I was doing Bill Manhire's Original Composition course in my second year at univer-sity. And, thirteen years later, a year before *The Vintner's Luck* appeared,

I began writing *Black Oxen*. So, *Black Oxen* is my favourite because it is the book based on my imaginary game that I was always trying to write. It's particularly about the game Sara, Madeline, Phillip and I played as university students in our flat on Kelburn Parade. When the characters in *Black Oxen* are nostalgic about living in the Presidential Palace after the revolution, that's me being nostalgic about that flat, and about the old museum on Buckle Street, where I worked – a labyrinthine building full of strange subterranean rooms. When *Black Oxen*'s people remember their wild youth – drug-taking, love affairs, hard work, factions, terrible betrayals – I'm remembering my twenties, how we'd be working or going to school, and to political meetings, and would still play late, till our voices were hoarse. We were haunted and intoxicated and out of our heads – in the heads of our characters. *Black Oxen* has all that, a feeling that people are possessed, and the whole world is haunted, and rationality is paper-thin.

Another reason that it's my favourite book is that it's the only one that took all my brain, all my attention, all my organisational skills to write. It gave my highly intelligent editor at FSG migraines when she was working on it (yet it's her favourite of the four books we did together). Actually, I have this memory of ringing her home on 9/11 to check on her and getting her husband. He told me that she was in transit from her office, walking blocks and blocks to pick up their kids from school. I got that out of him, then he wanted to talk about *Black Oxen*, which he just finished reading. There I was in Wellington, twitching with alarm and awe about world events, and he was in Manhattan, full of my mad book.

CD: When you attended Victoria University, you took a writing class with New Zealand poet, Bill Manhire. How significant has your relationship with other influential writers in New Zealand been to your own creative development?

EK: I would love to have had the opportunity to do the degree course in creative writing that Bill's International Institute of Modern Letters offers now. Back when I did Original Composition it was a six credit course in stage two English – a humble thing. But it was just what

I needed at the time. I'd written two novels already, and was full of ideas, but foundering, and discouraged, and unpublished (I was also only 23). Bill always treated me as if I was already a writer. He was right, only I had to learn how to get the saddle and bridle on my talent. The workshops were great for that – looking at what other writers were trying to do, learning how malleable thoughts and words were. Bill was good at picking people. Poet Jenny Bornholdt and playwright Ken Duncum were also in that year. And since Bill had kindly and foolishly let Sara and me into the course together (with ten others) the class quickly became rather informal.

Bill was my academic advisor. He had me dropping courses in later years so that I could finish the novel I started in the course. He took *After Z-Hour* to Victoria University Press, and introduced me to the press's editor, Fergus Barrowman – whom I married. (It is by no means sure that two shy and prickly people like Fergus and I would have managed to find one another even in Wellington if we didn't come with these mutual high recommendations by someone we trusted and looked up to.) Anyway, throughout the years Bill has always taken a warm interest in my work. And that's the thing. The so-called 'Wellington School' is actually just a group of writers who have taken a warm interest in one another's work. And it's a gestalt – together we have raised our game.

CD: Your most recent novel, *Dreamhunter*, is directed at young adults in addition to an adult readership. How was the process of writing for young adults different to previous writing you have done? Can you also comment on the use of fantastic naturalism in your work?

EK: I had to discover how I could do it, what my young adult book would be like. For me the difference was something to do with what Fergus refers to as the 'emotional temperature' of a book. One of the things that attracts me to young adult fiction as a reader is young adult books' lack of ironic distance. Which isn't to say that they lack irony, but they never seem to want to call attention to their own artifice. I dislike books where the author is determined to let the reader know that they know they are writing a book. It seems a very bossy, intrusive and insincere sort of abdication of authority. I guess I believe in Forster's idea that the author should be like God, present everywhere, and invisible. There are many young adult writers whose personalities are strongly present in their books, in the form of style and world view, but who would never dream of getting between the characters and the readers. This is the main thing I learned writing for young adults – as an author I was already nigh on invisible in my books, but I had also to learn how to be a better conduit. My English editor Julia Wells made this clear to me – the reader must always know what the main characters are thinking and feeling.

I'm trying to coin 'fantastic naturalism' as a description of what I do. My ghosts, golems, vampires and angels appear in worlds of closely observed reality. Magic realism always suggests fable to me. My books aren't fabulous in that sense. I'm interested in society, in families, in the real appearance of 'the world'. But I write fantasy. When my agent called my books 'Jane Austen with monsters' she hit the nail on the head, I think.

So, why do I write fantasy? The best answer is that – given my life, given the imaginary game – what other kind of writing would I do?

Because my father was a born-again atheist, and my mother a quietly definite unbeliever, when I was a child I had very firm ideas about what constituted crucial truths. I *knew* God did not exist. It had been handed down to me from on high – or rather from my father. Since the matter was settled, and I was safe from the error of belief and could play at seances but not get scared, I was left to discover for myself what would make my hair stand on end, what communicated awe or promised transfiguration. Not what was true, but what *felt* true.

I often think that fantasy appeals to young people because they have a sense that their worlds are still unstable and permeable, haven't yet hardened around them into the insistent reality of the everyday. Perhaps, too, raging hormones and rude good health can encourage the young to feel that something miraculous is about to happen – that they are close to a momentous transformation, that they are special, and the moon is a god in their heads. I felt like this day after day in my teens – crazy with life. This is the felt truth of much young adult fiction, whose heroes are often specially fated. And it isn't only young people who apprehend the world this way, adults often do too. Because of mass communications, we know so much now, and find it hard look at the horizon and wonder. We sometimes have to imagine that there are holes in our maps and that our map-makers are mistaken, or blind, or are perpetrators of *X-Files*-like conspiracies. We have a sense of something bigger, of some heroic, meaningful life happening just out of the corner of our eyes. A sense of something that, if we can only just chance on it, will remove us from our mundane, muggle lives, into a world where there are things that we *alone can do* – and where consciousness is an adventure.

The fantasy that I've loved – fantasy, science fiction, horror – has often been inspired by dread or longing. I believe we do sometimes feel that we have an antisocial other self who has inhuman energy, a Mr Hyde bristling within our civil skins. And we do sometimes imagine that by some appalling mischance we might wake up on the operating table – or in our graves like the poor people in Poe's stories. And we do feel grief when the elves go west at the end of *Lord of the Rings*. And we do feel grief for Susan, lost in the world of lipsticks and nylons, and lost to Peter and Edmund and Lucy, who are happy in the heaven of the Lion.

The energy in all these stories comes from things we feel are true. Does fantasy address life? Perhaps not – but only if we are somehow more *ourselves* at forty than at fourteen.

---

* **Denis Glover** (1912–80), poet, printer, publisher, satirist, sailor and boxer; he wrote 'The Magpies' which has to be New Zealand's most famous poem. There is a *Selected Poems* (1996) compiled by Bill Manhire. **Noel Hilliard** (1929–97) was a major novelist of the 1960s, now fallen somewhat into neglect. His best known book is *Maori Girl* (1960). **Sam Hunt** (1946–), poet and performer, and one of New Zealand's most recognisable figures. A man who brought poetry to the people. Sam lived for years at 'bottle creek' in Paremata. **Ian Cross** (1925–) is known as author of *The God Boy* and other novels and as a distinguished journalist, editor and executive manager. He was editor of the *Listener* at the time of that hangi.

Jenny Bornholdt
The Rocky Shore

Monday morning and I want to paint the shed,
but it's Room Two at the rocky shore.

Children in their named sunhats, with buckets,
clamber around the rocks, poke at things – starfish,

anemones, the odd unfortunate crab. It's rocky
and it's the shore, and very bright. The hem of my skirt

is wet and really, my mind's on other things. Like the afternoon's
translation seminar, which is where I eventually drive to,

brushing sand from my hair; and then I am in the lecture theatre
with my still-damp salty clothes, trying to translate myself

from the rocky shore to here, to the shed, where the paint waits,
viscous in every language.

———

Home is a house of men. Men I love, but what I crave
is a shed. I always thought I should have been

a boy. I liked girls, but I liked boys better. That's
changed now, though I still envy them their shirts.

My friend, Peter, has about sixty. All second-hand.
We spent a morning once, speculating on their previous

lives and decided that maybe there should be some kind of quarantine
station for old shirts, so they could get their old inhabitants

out of their systems. About this time, people started mistaking me
for a doctor. A woman even came up to me at a party and asked

if I was a psychiatrist. Peter, my friend with the shirts,
suggested that I might just have that look about me.

Anyway, this doctor thing was unusual (I could be more
literary and say *resonant*) because for years I did want

to be a doctor, but never felt able. From time to time I still entertain
thoughts of medicine. Usually when I read about doctors saving lives

(this appeals to my sense of the heroic), or we need to buy a new
heat exchanger for the caliphont.

———

A shed seemed a desirable structure, so my friend, Chris, drew
one up, and I made the shape out of an old sheet and

sailed it around the lawn at the back of our house. This part of our garden
was a place I didn't visit much after my father died. He and my

mother and Greg and the children and I had spent a lot of time
up there, clearing and digging, and when my father became ill

we closed it down. Lay newspapers and flattened boxes over the earth
and abandoned it to itself. I've already written a poem, some poems,

about this and don't want to repeat myself. But then I do.
People often ask about the *form* of a poem and I usually say something like

the poem finds its own form. Which is something I believe. Truly.
But sometimes it takes a while. This poem, for instance, was like the shed.

I had to make it out of something and move it around the lawn. I didn't
want to repeat myself, but then I did. The garden needed revisiting.

No two sheds are ever the same.

———

Margaret rings. Suggest a yard full of previous habitation. Doors stacked –
framed, unframed, the occasional cracked pane. He's coming through, she's

gone, she's slammed the door, there was no need for that.
Bent back through a window, she watches, sees the blossom full

of bees. Chris says *you know if you choose these windows
you'll be building a window, not a shed.* The man in the yard says

*she may well be a poet, but the only writing of hers I'm interested in seeing
is on a cheque.*

———

Monday morning I arrive home to find a truck outside, and on it
half the six-paned bow window. The other half rests on our front porch.

That night a great wind shakes the garden. In the morning
the shed, still a sheet, is wrapped around a tree. What began as

talk, then pencil marks on paper, a sheet on the ground, a wrapped
tree, becomes four walls and a roof in the minds of our builders

who arrive and walk the steps up to the top garden. As they head
up, our child descends into illness. His first steady translation of

one thing into another.

――――

For a whole day, the apprentice named Jessie
carted bags of cement mix and wood up to the back lawn.

He was a procession of one, back and forth past the kitchen
window. A boy of few words that became fewer

as the day wore on, he also became smaller, bowed down, as he was,
by the load. As the materials gathered on the grass, I moved the trees.

――――

The garden, you see (and must understand) is a mess. This is no
false modesty. Once a newspaper did a story on me and my

garden, thinking, mistakenly, that because I write about gardens,
I know what I am talking about. I explained my position and lack

of expertise, but they persisted, and because I was a nicer person
then than I am now, I gave in. To my alarm, a day later, there was
a message

from a photographer saying would this afternoon suit? A nice guy,
he came down the front path, looked around and said *Jesus*.

——

In an odd place in the lawn is a lovely old apple blossom, which looks
like snow from the kitchen window. I'd planted a fig, olive and bay

in memory of Mary Ursula Bethell. Of course these were the first trees
that had to be moved. You think you have everything in its right place

and bingo, something goes and blows it all apart. I had taken
this garden apart once, and here I was doing it again. Still left

is the pale yellow dog rose, backdrop to the new black doris plum,
planted because that was my grandmother's name. The mother

of my father. Sometimes I would like the garden to just be
the garden and not a place of memory. I moved the fig

and olive, left the bay as a cornerstone for the shed
and forgot the old rose. Days later I found it replanted

beside the plum. Now it's called *the builders' rose*. Why this need
to name and place everything? I do the same with clothing –

always want to give its genealogy. *New trousers?* asks
my sister, raising an eyebrow. *Yes*, I reply. *Four dollars*

from the Salvation Army in Newtown. What do you think? Fine,
just don't wear them out anywhere.

Once the builders had moved the rose, they dug deep into the generous,
forgiving earth, then laid the foundations. Concrete slab like a sheet.

————

While the men build, I tend to our sick child who moves
further and further into an illness constructed from grief and

loss. Even as I write these words I feel uncomfortable. Show
not tell, is the way, I know, but in this case I want to say. *Grief*

and loss. And again. *Grief and loss.* As the men build on the back
lawn, where the boy remembers his grandfather, he too constructs

his own shelter. Illness his shed, or place of retreat.

————

One of the builders' vans breaks down and down, then our car too
breaks down in Cuba Street. I walk around the corner to Driscolls,

ask Les for help and he leaves the car he's under and comes,
crowbar in hand. Lifts the bonnet and shows me the place to

give it a tap. Things you can fix by knocking. Fords, says Les,
they often have a problem with the dash lights. *You just*

give the dash a bit of a knock and on they'll go.

————

My sister's baby. Her heartbeat dropped down
and down and a cry went up and the baby was delivered just

in time. As I write that, my sister walks past on the road below,
pushing the baby in her pram. Looks up and waves. *Look,*

here comes the mother of someone, says our youngest son
on the way to school. And there goes the mother of our friends.

Her two sons polish their shoes on the verandah in their under-
wear on the morning of her funeral. White boxers, roses,

sheet; clean black shoes. Nails knocked into the coffin.
And then the danger begun, writes our son.

———

Is your kid still sick? asks Jessie.
He's not gonna die, is he?

Scaffolding up around the school holidays.

*It would be sad if you died because you wouldn't get
to go through all the numbers.*

———

I spend a lot of time at the dentists and the hospital.
One child has a supernumerary tooth holed up in his gum.

It stops his big front tooth making its way into the world. The gap
has been there since we were in Menton, France, two years ago,

and has come to resemble that place we miss most. The other child
develops a tooth abscess, which, until we spend an afternoon

up at the hospital, is not deemed to be urgent. Then it is.
We drive to Keneperu Hospital very early one morning in fog.

He has a long wait, an iceblock, and two hours
in a laz-y-boy, before driving home again. Weird ways

to spend your days. *This is a grand and hallowed moment*
says the child, as she kicks off into the pool.

———

Our friend Noel, who is always drinking something
new and interesting, is having trouble with his kiln,

hence the Hindu blessing. He writes, enclosing copies
of the instructions: Dear Noel,

thanks for inviting me to consecrate your kiln
herewith are the things you will need to purchase:

VASHTU SHANTI CEREMONY
coconuts small x 2
bananas x 10
seasonal fruit
fresh dates x 100gms
turmeric powder x 50gms
flowers x 4 bunches
rice (white) x 1kg
matches or lighter x 1
incense sticks x 1 pkt

Dollar coins (washed) x 5

ADDITIONAL REQUIREMENTS

mango leaves – unblemished – x 10

trays and vessels (brass, copper, steel)

new tea towels OR 1 roll paper towels

INSTRUCTIONS

This ceremony is the traditional ceremony performed

for the sanctification of the home or business to generate

a peaceful and harmonious environment in which to live

and to prosper. I will arrive half an hour before the puja –

please have all the puja items ready as per the list – all fruit

to be washed. The family should take a bath before the ceremony

and wear clean clothes. Loose fitting white clothes for men are preferable

and coloured for ladies. Jeans are not suitable. Explanations

will be given in English before and during the ceremony.

All chatting and gossiping is to be avoided so that those who are serious

can concentrate fully on the puja. Please note: Until now

we have avoided setting fees for pujas, since it is our sacred duty and not

our business. But due to the fact that some hosts have been

unfair in their charity, indifferent to the value of our time
and unmindful of the cost of living to which we are subjected,

we are now compelled to set a minimum donation of $150
per ceremony. Thank you for your patronage.
Rami.

Shortly after the blessing,
Noel's kiln exploded.

———

I have become a woman who walks. People assume I must think
about things – poetry maybe – (I blame Wordsworth for this) but no,

I pride myself on thinking about nothing in particular, just try
     to concentrate
on each step on the ground and look around. The other day though,

I found myself puzzling over *Swedish rounding* at the supermarket.
I enjoy the snatches of conversation – two cyclists: *You know what*
     they say,

if you're thirsty it's too late. And the boy talking to himself: *There is*
     much similarity
between station wagons, more variety is what's needed.

———

Walls laid, then raised against the cold light of the garden.
The shed's articulation. We stand in the skeleton of the doorway

and look out on the lawn's other structure. A rabbit cage.
We have become a foster home for hedgehogs. Hedgehogs?

Well you might ask. The SPCA asks will we be okay to administer
medicine should they need it? *Medicine? What kind of medicine?*

Well, they get mange sometimes. Oh. And what sort of medication
might they need for that? Well, it's sheep dip. But you only give them

a tiny bit.

The 'O' in the centre of your name, says Denis O'Connor, you work
from there.

——

Children play. *Say you be the bad guy and I'll be in here in the fort*
and you have to attack me. Yeah and say I come in here with my

guys and we'll do a raid and say we have secret weapons. Yeah and
say I blast you before you shoot off your secret weapons and say

you lose them and say my guys capture them and then we have
a battle about the weapons. Yeah and say then you get injured

and your guys have to come and rescue you. And say a child
is troubled and nothing seems to help and you don't know what to do?

What then?

——

Send a postcard to Noel to check about the kiln. He rings
to say actually it was a fault with the glaze.

The supplier kept saying *just try it at a higher temperature*
so he did and eventually this caused a meltdown in the kiln.

So it wasn't the fault of the kiln blesser. Maybe it was because
the supplier hadn't been blessed.

God will bless you, says Bill as he hammers in
another nail.

It's important to get the facts right, says Noel. Every day
that passes, events become more hazy. This

according to a forensics programme he's been watching
on television. A day can make all the difference.

In between episodes, Noel has been painting the most
commonly caught fish in Australia. Murray Cod

is a huge river fish, caught most successfully using
a scorched *starling* as bait. How did anyone discover that?

——

Pioneer Red walls go all around and then the roof is on.
I buy beer to celebrate. *Just whatever's cheapest*, says Bill.

We raise a branch above the roof to mark the days when trees
were the highest things on the land, then raise our glasses to the shed.

———

As an antidote to exams, our tallest son (the one the youngest calls
boy-man), sets a small plane on a round-the-world flight on his computer.

Comes upstairs to tell us he's over Greece, then has to leave
because he's about to attempt his first night landing.

Downstairs there's engine trouble over Athens.
There might be a question about moral necessity.

———

They make good the walls, the men. They make it all
good, and then they go. Down the steps. Leave the shed

behind them. My shed. And the scaffolding. We like these men,
we are sad to see them go. Pioneer Red and Manuka Honey

on the outside. Pioneer Red floor, Jungle Mist walls on the inside.
After trying Rivendell, Laurel, Bush, English Holly and Heather.

Each week, as I paint,
our son invents a new illness.

The garden too, made good. You don't want to repeat yourself
but then you do. The child digs for the chink

of metal on stone and goes down to discover the path
which became buried and turned to grass. Move the lilac.

Revive the olive. Bay thankfully thrives at the corner.
Plant raspberry canes where the gooseberries used to be. Leave

the rhododendron and the rose. Move the lemon to where at last
it looks convincing.

――――

After the storm, blossoms stuck to the window
like confetti. We're about to go to Waitarere Beach

and my mother tells me the last time she was there
was with my father, the weekend before their wedding.

The two of them went with friends and sat on the sand
talking about the future. The future. Here we are in it,

some of us, some of us not.

――――

I miss my father.
I miss having a father.

――――

Why didn't you let me visit him when he was dying?
Why didn't we let him visit when he was dying?

A question like the path, uncovered. Because I didn't know
how. There seemed no hope in it. Death seemed such unfair knowledge

for a child to have. And I am sorrier than I can ever say. Although I do,
over and over, and hope that having uncovered this path,

which leads nowhere in the garden, but to the bedside of what
troubles him, I can show I didn't mean harm.

———

This morning, on the waterfront, the couple who run
bound at the wrist. After a few mornings I realised

he was blind. She talks him through it. *The sky
is lightening. It's very calm and beautiful.*

Do you think it's going to be a good day?
Yes, I think it is.

Jenny Bornholdt has published seven books of poetry, including a selected
poems, *Miss New Zealand*. Her most recent collection is *Summer* (Victoria
University Press), written in 2002 while she was the Katherine Mansfield
Memorial Fellow in Menton, France. She is co-editor of *An Anthology of New
Zealand Poetry* (Oxford University Press).

Peter Christiansen

The White Woman of Gippsland

Peter Christiansen, a
Victorian teacher
librarian, is the author
of *People of the Merri
Merri* and a contributor
to the recently
published *Encyclopedia
of Melbourne*.

In the summer of 1840, a large body of Kulin comprising elements of the Wurundjeri and Bunurong peoples left Melbourne, travelled down the eastern peninsula bordering Port Phillip Bay, camped for a while near a chain of waterholes in the proximity of the landmark hill named Arthur's Seat, then made the decision to separate and broke into smaller groups. The Aboriginal protectors appointed to the Port Phillip region had been instructed to itinerate with the indigenous people placed in their care. William Thomas was under orders always to follow the largest indigenous band, which at that moment happened to be a section of the Bunurong numbering approximately fifty-seven individuals. When the protector joined this gathering he encountered an atmosphere of tension that had nothing to do with the breaking of government promises or the shortage of food rations. A Wurundjeri headman issued Thomas with a warning recorded in the protector's diary in which he wrote he had been 'told very hard, not to follow that lot, I should be killed'.

Nevertheless, despite the sense of mystery, Thomas and the Bunurong travelled safely across the peninsula to Western Port Bay and on the surface all seemed well. In early February 1840 having manoeuvred a cumbersome bullock dray across five muddy creek beds they arrived at Yallock station, home to the squatter Robert Jamieson. Thomas and Jamieson were well acquainted having travelled out from England together on the same immigrant ship. Jamieson's workers and the Kulin mixed together in a relaxed friendly manner with the station hands spending much of one warm summer's day swimming with the Bunurong girls in the Yallock creek. At night, in front of roaring bonfires Thomas conducted a religious service in which the Kulin joined with the Europeans in singing extracts from the Hallelujah chorus and a selection of popular hymns. The Aboriginal people were fascinated by the sound of European music and the singing of sacred songs initially attracted many Kulin to church services in Melbourne. Along the frontier settlers were often startled by the ability of clans people to provide unexpected but accurate renditions of traditional Scottish ballads.

In the course of this journey Thomas learnt about the long-standing conflict between the Kulin clans of Melbourne and their *meymet* foes. When asked the meaning of the word 'meymet', the Kulin said this dismissive term was best translated into English by the phrase, 'wild blackfellows'. The meymet included all people from distant clans who lay outside the bonds of kinship. The Kulin were longstanding enemies of the Kurnai, the Aboriginal people who occupied the region well to the east of the township of Melbourne. Separated by differences in language and custom, Kulin and Kurnai at this stage of their history had no connection through marriage. Attacks and counterattacks formed part of an ancient feud that had begun long before the appearance of white settlers.

Warawdor, a senior clan elder informed Thomas a party of Bunurong men would be away for some time on a hunting trip to the Dandenong Ranges collecting *Bullin Bullin* or lyrebird feathers for sale in the Melbourne market. In reality these men had formed themselves into a war party and were preparing to launch an assault on Kurnai territory. In order to avoid suspicion, Bunurong warriors had hidden sharpened pieces of thick glass in their kangaroo skin bags. On leaving camp they attached these glass barbs to their wooden spear shafts turning them into deadly weapons. A Kulin war party, wrote Thomas, in the notes prepared for a book on the Aborigines that was destined to remain unpublished, was prepared to endure intense fatigue and hardship in order to avenge past wrongs.[i] Once they crossed into the country of their enemies, Kulin warriors were required to exercise great caution and discipline when it came to securing game. It was far too dangerous, said Thomas, to wake up the bush with the noise of a full-scale kangaroo hunt, so the raiders lived on smaller animals such as bandicoot and possum, supplementing their diet with grubs and wattle gum. At various times of the day the warriors walked backwards to mislead enemy trackers as to the direction they were taking. The war party would halt just before sunset to collect leaves, sticks and bark strips which they used to fuel a series of small fires, deftly made to produce minimal smoke and flame. One or two men were selected to keep watch throughout the night while their comrades slept. When morning came the raiders carefully extinguished their fires, buried their excrement and disguised their campsite by spreading dry leaves over cold embers and ash. The war party travelled as far as the Snowy River where they came across a group of Kurnai men, women and children. The Kulin staged an ambush, slaughtered many, cut strips of flesh from the bodies of the fallen and removed their victims' *marmbula*, or kidney fat. According to Warawdor, the marmbula, prized as a mystical source of strength was extracted after making an incision in a person's flank, thrusting one's fingers into the opening, locating the kidneys and yanking them out of the body while chanting ritual phrases over the dying foe.

In their encampment close by Jamieson's station the Bunurong women, longing for their absent men, would gather in the afternoon an hour before sunset, turn their faces to the east, the direction taken by the raiding party and send a great shout echoing through the bush. Through the force of their lungs and the assistance of friendly spirits they broadcast a message of support to their absent warriors. It was the sound of female voices that woke Thomas well before daybreak on the morning of Monday 9 March 1840, as he heard the Bunurong women joyfully welcome back their Kulin after an absence of twenty-three days. Several men limped into camp utterly exhausted having completed the last stage of their journey without food or sleep. When questioned by Thomas the Bunurong denied at first making any attack on the meymet, but in the coming weeks the true story of their raid gradually emerged.

Eight months later, Kurnai fighters searching for the raiders who had attacked them in the summer, traced the tracks of their enemies to Robert Jamieson's Yallock station. On Saturday 3 October 1840 a horde of angry warriors, shaking weapons and shouting at the top of their voices stormed Jamieson's homestead. The attackers smashed windows, ransacked huts, chased Irish farmhands into the creek, tore up bedding and trashed the station's library. Robert Jamieson grabbed one gun, fired it into the air and then aimed a second loaded rifle directly at the rampaging warriors. The Kurnai paid him not the slightest attention. Jamieson would say later, he might as well have pointed a walking stick at them for all the good it did. In spite of the fear, tension and property damage neither side was willing to shed blood. No European was speared or hacked with a tomahawk, and in return no shots were fired at the raiders. After several hours of intimidation, destruction and looting the attackers abruptly departed.

Western Port lay within Thomas's jurisdiction and the protector hurried to investigate the assault on Jamieson's station, believing he should be the one to initiate contact with the Kurnai rather than relying on a display of goodwill from a detachment of soldiers. Two young Bunurong men elected to travel with Thomas and help guide him through the bush. At the start of their pursuit there was initially no great mystery as to the direction taken by the departing Kurnai warriors. Even William Thomas could follow the trail of ripped up bedding, scattered pillow feathers, broken china, torn newspapers, discarded tin dishes and quantities of tea and flour strewn through the scrub. Thomas and his Bunurong trackers soon came upon a native camp hidden close to the Jamieson homestead. The trackers knelt to examine the ground outside a series of abandoned bark shelters as they could tell by the pressure marks left on the grass how many people had been present in each *miam*. No one had slept the night before the attack, they declared. The Kurnai warriors had spent their time restlessly pacing backwards and forwards or squatting by one of the eighteen small fires they had lit. The evidence gleaned from the campsite suggested Jamieson and his men had been under close observation for some days, indicating the attack on the station was a well-planned event and not a spontaneous act of rage.

The trail led away from the base camp and came to what Thomas termed grotesque wooden monuments, carved out of living trees and fallen timber. A line of thin saplings had been bent over and their tops secured to the ground with grass ropes forming a succession of shallow arches. A series of larger, older trees had been deliberately cut and notched, their upper branches removed and used to form patterns on the ground. This work had apparently been performed with a cross saw taken from Jamieson's property.

As he was about to pitch his tent for the night Thomas discovered a second grove of gum saplings, cut and shaped by Aboriginal hands wielding a European axe and saw. An ancient tree stump had been decorated with pieces of fresh foliage tied to its base by lengths of native rope manufactured out of strands of twisted bark. In the morning close by his tent door, he found a strange collection of thin branches, stripped of leaves and pushed into the ground to form a tight grove of wooden pillars, standing about ten feet tall. His Kulin companions professed ignorance of the customs of their enemies and were unable or unwilling to explain what these sculpted trees might mean. Thomas, eager to continue the hunt, lost the support of his trackers, who pointed out that the Kurnai, for their own unfathomable reasons, might be willing to spare European lives, but there was no reason to think this amnesty would be extended to their Kulin foes. In the interests of their own safety, they insisted on calling off the pursuit.

The leaders of two rival exploration parties, Angus Macmillan, a Scottish pastoralist and Paul Strezlecki, a Polish adventurer, are credited as the pathfinders who opened up the lands of the Kurnai, a great expanse of mountain, forest, lake and river in the eastern region of Port Phillip, to European settlement. Both Strezlecki and Macmillan relied on Aboriginal guides to help them navigate their way through difficult and heavily forested terrain. Both men were active name-givers, who did their best to ensure the map of this district read like a well-established province of Greater Britain. The chain of sizable lagoons bounded by the ninety-mile beach and traditional food resource for the Kurnai, became known as Lake Wellington, Lake Victoria and Lake King. The rivers watering this area lost their local titles and became known instead as the Mitchell, the Macallister and the Nicholson with only the Tambo retaining some vestige of indigenous origins. Strezlecki was responsible for naming the entire district when he tactfully proposed calling this region Gippsland in honour of His Excellency Sir George Gipps, the governor of New South Wales.

Angus Macmillan made his own distinctive contribution to history in a letter published by the *Sydney Herald* in late December 1840. Macmillan had been travelling through Gippsland with a group of pastoralists when he disturbed a native encampment by the banks of a river he had called the Glengarry but which Strezlecki had more successfully named the La Trobe after the Superintendent commanding the colony at Port Phillip. The moment the Aborigines caught sight of Macmillan's party they fled into the bush. An examination of their deserted huts revealed a range of European artefacts including check shirts, moleskin trousers smeared with human blood, women's apparel, a child's white frock, ten new English blankets, shoemakers' awls, bottles of all descriptions and a selection of London, Glasgow and Aberdeen newspapers dating back several years. The remains of a two-year-old male child, found wrapped inside three kangaroo skin bags were examined by Macmillan's companion Dr Arbuckle, who declared the deceased child was undoubtedly the offspring of European parents. The belief quickly formed in Macmillan's mind that he had come across the aftermath of a dreadful massacre perpetrated by the Gippsland blacks. When he had first approached the encampment he had seen men with spears shepherding a number of women away and he had noticed how one particular female had looked back over her shoulder at him. Macmillan said he had thought little of this at first but after examining the contents of the native huts he now decided the 'unfortunate female' he had glimpsed was in fact a white woman and she was being held captive by a band of 'ruthless savages'.[2]

Macmillan's letter reprinted in the Melbourne press in January 1841 under the headline SUPPOSED OUTRAGE BY BLACKS attracted only minimal attention among the Port Phillip settlers because included in the long list of goods found in the Kurnai camp was a hand towel embroidered with the name *R Jamieson*. The Melbourne colonists believed the goods discovered in the Gippsland encampment had been stolen from Jamieson's station and could not be used to corroborate the claim a party of shipwrecked Europeans had been massacred by the Kurnai. This meant of course, the captured white woman was a figment of Macmillan's overwrought imagination, which was under some duress due to the length of time he had spent in the bush deprived of female companionship.

The story of a white woman surviving a shipwreck on the Gippsland coast only to fall into hands of wild, uncivilised blacks was too good a tale to be subverted by a lack of factual evidence. Rumours of a white female residing with an Aboriginal tribe persisted, fuelled by the occasional letter in the colonial press from anonymous correspondents, demanding urgent action be taken to retrieve the missing woman. Six years after Macmillan made his initial claim there was an upsurge in fresh sightings of a European female being held hostage by the Aborigines. These new reports were treated seriously by the colonial government despite the fact or indeed because of the fact they were provided by Aboriginal eyewitnesses.

In March 1846 a unit of native police, formed from Kulin volunteers was stationed in Gippsland patrolling Angus Macmillan's pastoral station in a bid to curb the activities of Kurnai cattle spearers. Trooper Quandite claimed he saw a 'yellow woman' with shoulder-length brown hair step out of her possum skin rug, then disappear naked into the bush hustled away by her black companions. Watched by his fellow troopers Quandite picked up her discarded possum skin cloak, held it up to his face and declared the human scent clinging to the fur confirmed it had been recently worn by a white woman. Hamilton Walsh, the European commander of Quandite's unit had seen nothing at all and he questioned the black trooper as to why had he not rushed over and rescued this female. Quandite replied he was so astounded by the sight of a white woman in the bush he had been unable to act and by the time he recovered his senses she had vanished. Quandite's statement was strongly supported by his fellow troopers. The native police were quite familiar with the notion of a white women being held hostage by 'wild blackfellows' having previously investigated sightings of her in the Wimmera to the north-west of Melbourne, Portland Bay to the south-west and now in Gippsland to the east.

Another key Aboriginal witness now came to the attention of the authorities in the form of a ten-year-old Kurnai boy who had attached himself to a Gippsland pastoralist. Known by the name Jacka-wadden he had resisted attempts to return him to is own people, declaring it was his intention to 'stop a while with the whites'. After living on a pastoral station for six months he was sufficiently confident of his command of English to tell anyone who cared to listen that a white woman was living with his tribe. Curiously Jacka-wadden claimed he had never actually seen this woman but had spent time playing with her half-caste children on the occasion of their visit to one of the native encampments.

Charles Tyers, the Commissioner for Crown Land in Gippsland, was excited by these reports and he wrote to inform his superior, Charles La Trobe, of these promising developments in the case of the missing white woman. Prior to the appearance of Jacka-wadden there had been minimal communication between the European and the Kurnai communities, said Tyers, and this young boy represented a chance to open up a dialogue with the indigenous people of Gippsland. The Kurnai probably had good reason to fear and avoid the European settlers. Most Gippsland pastoralists claimed Scottish ancestry and they were enraged when the body of one of their compatriots, Ronald Macalister, was found lying in a paddock, hacked to pieces by the Gippsland blacks. It is commonly believed Angus Macmillan led Gippsland's expatriate highlanders in a series of retaliatory raids that led to the slaughter of a great many Kurnai. A paucity of documentary evidence makes it difficult to evaluate the extent and intensity of this conflict but it does explain the fear many Kurnai had of the settlers.[3]

Tyers thought the best way to retrieve the woman was to culti-vate the Kurnai using Jacka-wadden as a go-between, offering gifts of blankets and other items in a trust-building exercise. If this approach failed, then the only alternative, claimed Tyers, was to send in armed police to scour the countryside even though he acknowledged this latter strategy was likely to result in bloodshed. Superintendent

La Trobe wrote back to Tyers approving of his plan to use moderate means to investigate the whereabouts of Quandite's 'yellow woman' and to strive to obtain the trust and cooperation of the Kurnai. On his inspection tour of Gippsland during the previous year La Trobe had made his own enquiries into the origin of the white woman rumour. After questioning 'the gentlemen of the district' in regard to the story he conceded the possibility there might have been a Caucasian female living with an Aboriginal tribe in years gone by. However, in recent times there had been a great deal of European movement and activity throughout Gippsland and no message, sign or communication in regard to the white woman had managed to reach the ears of the settlers. Even though it seemed highly improbable La Trobe was prepared to entertain the possibility that a white female had indeed survived a shipwreck and was now cohabiting with the Gippsland blacks. However, after enduring so many years of obvious 'degradation' this female might now prefer to remain in the company of the natives or as the Superintendent put it, be 'indifferent or adverse to reclamation by those of her own race'. La Trobe urged Tyers to proceed with the 'greatest caution and prudence' and on no account was he to endanger anyone's life including that of the alleged female captive by risking a violent confrontation with the natives.[4]

Police parties made four separate journeys into the bush and spent a total of thirty-one days looking for the elusive white female. Jacka-wadden's tribe were tracked from their home by Lake Wellington up to the Snowy River, a distance of a hundred miles but no sign of any white hostage was discovered. The police did, however, receive more valuable information from helpful Aboriginal informants. They were told the white woman had been given the name Loondigon and she had been living for a number of years with Bungaleana, a man of some importance amongst the Kurnai, who guarded her jealously and kept her virtually as his prisoner.

In Melbourne newspaper proprietors were gripped with white-woman fever and they were thankful when even more black witnesses came forward with information which seemed to verify her existence. In August 1846 a Bunurong man named Yal Yal said to have been with Walsh in Gippsland claimed he knew all about the white woman.

On several occasions he had actually seen her footprints but following the rescue attempts undertaken by the police the Gippsland blacks had tied possum skins around her feet making it difficult to trace her. Yal Yal was living with a young woman he had obtained from Gippsland, and she claimed the white woman had given birth to several children while living with Bungaleana, was very unhappy and 'plenty cry'. William Thomas said when Yal Yal was directly questioned over his claims he became evasive and admitted his information had originated with another black in Gippsland. In regard to the account supplied by his female companion, he declared he was unable to understand a word she said because the Kurnai girl only 'spoke Irish'. These equivocations did little to dampen the zeal of the true believers keen to venture into the bush, locate the white woman and return her to civilisation.

At a public meeting held in September 1846 the citizens of Melbourne were asked to reflect on the horror of an educated white female, forcibly detained by a savage black cannibal, her misery and wretchedness only amplified by what were now surely bitter recollections of her former happy home. The meeting was told there was no doubt as to the authenticity of the reports in regard to this hapless female. The name of a European woman had been seen carved into the bark of a tree in an area unfrequented by white men. Reports furnished by Aboriginal witnesses were now being supplemented by statements supplied by respectable European colonists. A number of Gippsland settlers claimed they too had caught brief glimpses of a pale-skinned female flitting through the bush who always managed to disappear before they could intervene and rescue her.

Funds were raised to mount a private expedition to journey into Gippsland to locate and retrieve the wretched white prisoner. The expedition party would be led by Christiaan DeVilliers who some years previously had commanded an earlier version of the native police corps. Six white men as well as ten Aborigines drawn mainly from the ranks of the Bunurong people volunteered to accompany DeVilliers into Gippsland.

The Kulin encampments around Melbourne were virtually unhinged with excitement, wrote Thomas in his dairy, at the thought of going in pursuit of the white woman. The protector experienced feelings of trepidation when he saw Warawdor, Little Benbow, Yal Yal,

Charly, Toby, Teram, Mungerim, Tollert and two unnamed others preparing to board the steamship Shamrock which would transport them to the Gippsland coast. The men assembled wearing red woollen jackets, sturdy fustian trousers, new leather footwear and canvas knapsacks containing blankets strapped to their shoulders, leaving their hands free to cradle their firearms. Protector Thomas no doubt recalled what happened the last time Warawdor organised a party of warriors to venture into Kurnai territory. He made a point of lecturing the Kulin on the importance of ensuring no harm came to 'the poor Gippsland Blacks', and he wrote in his diary that the armed party had at least made a great show of listening to him. Thomas sought and was given assurances by DeVilliers that the expedition party would be scrupulous in ensuring no harm befell either the Kulin volunteers or the natives of Gippsland. The expedition leaders would follow La Trobe's cautious approach and try to win the friendship of the 'Warrigals' as they termed the Kurnai, fearing any act of violence might lead to the total disappearance of the woman or even provoke her death at the hands of her black oppressors.

The private expedition assisted by Warawdor and his companions came to Lake King and made contact with the local Kurnai people, who freely admitted a white woman was indeed living with Bungaleana, and he was unwilling to give her up. The Kurnai hummed a tune they had heard the woman sing and several Warrigals volunteered to lead the expedition party into the mountains to meet with Bungaleana and his female companion. DeVilliers accepted their offer but his guides disappeared once he entered the hill country, forcing him to retreat back to the lakes. DeVilliers wrote the captive woman a letter telling her a number of parties were actively searching for her and he enclosed a small lead pencil so she could write a response. Several Kurnai promised to smuggle the note to the woman and to ensure they did so unobserved by Bungaleana. Some days later they told DeVilliers the white woman had read his letter, which had provoked a great outpouring of tears. She was in the act of writing a reply when Bungaleana snatched the pencil out of her hand, nearly breaking her arm in the process, and told her he would not let her 'yabber with white fellows'.

Warawdor and his men worked hard to build a relationship with their one-time enemies. Corroborees were danced, joint hunting parties organised and expressions of goodwill were exchanged. DeVilliers recognised the efforts of his trackers and heaped praise on his Aboriginal aides. However, while the Kulin were building bridges with the Kurnai they were encountering difficulties with their friends and relatives serving with the native police. A group of Kurnai women who had been living with the native police for a number of months abruptly abandoned the troopers in order to partner Warawdor's men. The offering of women as sexual partners within indigenous societies was a means of establishing friendly relations with parties of strangers. The black police, unhappy with the loss of their female companions, convinced their commander Hamilton Walsh to pursue the issue on their behalf. Walsh spoke to Commissioner Tyers, saying he was concerned for the wellbeing of the women who had deserted his men and moved in with DeVilliers's trackers. The white officers acceded to the request of the troopers and ordered the women to return to the native police barracks, claiming this was the only way to ensure their safety.

After many unrewarding weeks of waiting, searching and listening to misleading claims, word finally reached Tyers that Bungaleana and his female prisoner were to be found by the banks of the Snowy River. Hamilton Walsh set out with a mixture of black and white troopers to investigate the report, closely followed by the private expedition force. When DeVilliers and his party arrived at the Snowy River they came across the aftermath of a recent fight between the Kurnai and the police. The body of a man with gunshot wounds and a smashed skull was found lying in the bush and a frightened Kurnai couple who had managed to escape police custody while chained by the ankle were located and set free. After undertaking a reconnoitre of the bush the expedition party came across a recently abandoned native encampment containing up to eight dead bodies.

DeVilliers hurried back to the headquarters of Charles Tyers located at Eagle Point overlooking Lake King and made a formal complaint regarding the conduct of the police. In subsequent letters to the press, members of the expedition described the Native Police as 'harpies from hell' who, with the connivance of the settlers, wrought death and destruction amongst the Gippsland blacks. Sergeant

McClelland, a European officer in the native police, wrote to the papers defending the black troopers against what he termed the falsehoods of the private expedition force. Only one native had died by the Snowy River said McClelland, and he had perished after a hand-to-hand struggle with a white trooper not a black one. According to McClelland the Gippsland blacks did not bury their dead but carried the bodies of their deceased about with them. The human remains found in the native encampment had been in various advanced stages of decomposition and while the cause of death was unknown they certainly had not died at the hands of the police.[5] However, the fact a confrontation had taken place at all, breached La Trobe's specific instructions to proceed with the greatest care and prudence. The native police were ordered by Tyers to confine themselves to their base, which left the pursuit of the white woman solely in the hands of the private expedition.

DeVilliers, having managed to sideline the native police, hurried to exploit his advantage. He returned to the Lakes region, gathered the Kurnai together and angrily told them their conduct was all 'gammon'. He was sick of their lies and misdirection and as a consequence he would head back to Melbourne, collect and arm the Whites and the Kulin and bring them back to punish the Gippslanders. These threats produced gratifying results as DeVilliers was immediately informed the white woman was now living in the mountains and there were any number of guides ready and willing to take him to her and assist in her recovery.

However, before they could proceed the Kurnai required DeVilliers and his party submit to a process of body painting. Black and white members of the expedition force removed their shirts and took off their trousers in order to apply thick streaks of ochre to their bare flesh. DeVilliers thought they all looked more than a little ludicrous but their marked skin satisfied the Kurnai request for a traditional, explicit sign of friendship. The expedition party encountered an estimated 220 Kurnai men, women and children camped by the banks of the Tambo River. The size of this gathering indicated the seriousness with which the Kurnai regarded the white woman business. DeVilliers and his fellow Europeans walked unarmed towards the Kurnai but they were not defenceless as their loaded guns, hidden behind a fallen log, were placed within easy reach of their Kulin scouts, all of whom were competent shots. The Kurnai made no attempt to deny the existence of the white woman and seemed, wrote DeVilliers, to take a certain boastful pride in having her in their possession. Some of the Kurnai women and children said the white woman was aware a party was out looking for her and often asked herself ' why did not the white men not come and fetch me away'. The expedition party was informed the female captive was sleeping only a short distance away and in the morning messengers carrying a freshly baked damper were despatched to collect her. DeVilliers and his men waited patiently all day but no one appeared. The next morning before sunrise, the Kurnai broke up their encampment and moved away, followed by the expedition party who caught up with them on the summit of a hilltop, where they accused the Warrigals of bad faith and treachery, and several scuffles broke out. After a tense standoff the Kurnai finally offered one of their own women to the expedition party but only on the condition that they were allowed to keep the captive white woman.

The expedition party returned to Melbourne empty-handed but declared their efforts had not been entirely in vain as the information they had gathered proved conclusively that a white woman was being held hostage by the Gippsland blacks. Two of the Kurnai guides who had been particularly cooperative also journeyed to Melbourne and spent several weeks living in the Kulin encampments near the main settlement. The *Port Phillip Herald*, the major financial sponsor of the expedition, thought this extraordinary display of conviviality between long-term enemies highlighted the leadership skills of Christian DeVilliers and his ability to command 'the passions of the natives'. William Thomas doubted the personal standing of one white officer would by itself be enough to stem a brutal vendetta that had lasted for many generations. He went to the Kulin encampments and spoke to the leading men, telling them if the Warrigals were killed they would all be deemed murderers and treated accordingly. The Kulin reassured the protector, telling him the Warrigals were safe from harm as they would never kill anyone who voluntarily placed themselves under their care.

The colonial government despatched one more search party into Gippsland only to find the local Aborigines were retracting their previous claims and now denied they had ever been in possession of a white female. Bungeleana went to the police, produced the woman called Loondigon and offered to hand her over even though it was obvious she was the offspring of Aboriginal parents. The Gippslanders then greatly tested the patience and credulity of the Europeans by claiming they had supposed all along the search parties were hunting for Loondigon, a Kulin woman who had been snatched from the Port Phillip district many years before.

Bungaleana was captured, brought before Commissioner Tyers and made to sign an agreement in which he promised to surrender the white woman in exchange for a supply of blankets and fishhooks. Having placed an 'X' on a formal agreement of understanding Bungaleana lead a police party into the mountains but he only made himself more unpopular with the whites when he failed to produce the alleged captive. Faced with the growing hostility of the authorities, Bungaleana agreed to lead the police to a secluded site by the lakes and hand over a prized artefact the Kurnai had kept hidden for years. He showed the whites a near life-sized female figure, with a red painted torso and white eyes that had once been attached to the prow of a shipwrecked coastal trader. Not surprisingly this third offer of a female failed to satisfy colonial official-dom and Bungaleana was removed from his own country and taken to the native police compound outside of Melbourne. He was kept chained to a tree until protector Thomas intervened and wrote to La Trobe complaining about his mistreatment. Bungaleana was never charged with an offence but he was kept in detention until the day he died as punishment for his role in either holding a white woman hostage or lying about doing so to the colonial authorities.

An Aboriginal man claiming to be Bungeleana's son visited Charles Tyers in November 1847 to report the death of the white woman. She had been crossing Lake King some months previously he said, when a sudden gale had blown up overturning her canoe and causing her to tumble into the water and drown. He body had been retrieved from the lake and placed in a hollow tree to decompose according to the funeral customs of the Kurnai. Tyers explored the boundaries of the lake, found no trace of a body, then sent for the native police, who soon returned to Eagle Point with a collection of human bones. The black police assured the Lands Commissioner he now had in his possession the mortal remains of the white woman and to support their claim they pointed out the skull they had presented him with was shaped differently to that of a black woman. As would be expected there were conflicting accounts as to the place, time and cause of the woman's death but the consensus view held the white woman was no longer among the living and no further search parties needed to be sent to Gippsland.

Police activity was halted but the Kulin continued to undertake their own journeys into Gippsland, seeking women. Colonisation had destroyed their traditional patterns of social exchange, forcing them to look far afield, even into the ranks of the 'wild blackfellows' to find suitable marriage partners. A year after the native police presented Tyers with a bundle of bones and a misshapen skull, William Thomas recorded thirteen Gippsland females partnering Kulin men in the Melbourne-Western Port region. These woman were obtained, wrote Thomas, through a mixture of seduction, barter, negotiation, and even though it was vigorously denied, armed extortion.[6] The Aborigines exploited the fable of a captive white woman to initiate peace negotiations between one time enemies, to facilitate the exchange of emissaries and quite possibly to deliberately torment and frustrate the white colonists.

Notes

[1] The journey to Arthur's Seat, Jamieson's station and description of the raiding party come from Thomas Papers MSS 214/3 and MSS 214/2, Mitchell Library.

[2] Macmillan's letter reproduced in Julie Carr's *The Captive White Woman of Gipps Land: In Pursuit of the Legend* (Melbourne, Melbourne Univ. Press, 2001).

[3] Don Watson's *Caledonia Australis* (Sydney, Collins, 1984) and Peter Gardner's *Our Founding Murdering Father* (Ensay, P. Gardner, 1987).

[4] Statements by Quandite, La Trobe, Tyers and police from the *William Cuthill manuscript*, State Library of Victoria.

[5] DeVilliers's letter *Port Phillip Herald* 11 February 1847, McClelland's letter *Port Phillip Patriot* 16 February 1847.

[6] Kurnai women with the Kulin, William Thomas Letter Books MSS 214/12 Mitchell Library. In 1850 Quandite, who had done more than most to spark the white woman mania, was ambushed by a group of aggrieved Kurnai by the banks of the Mitchell River and was fortunate to escape with his life.

Meredith Wattison
Egyptian Cotton

This is a day
when all walking women
look like you.
They have that same
mild, generic purpose
and self-effacement
you had.
They walk without a sense
of self,
as though bodiless.
They wear your clothes.
They carry letters to send.
Purse in their hand like a brick.
You walked past my window
several times today.
Just once I saw a wing's tip
slip from your sleeve,
feather like bread's loose wrap.
You winked at me.
Your grave was covered with flowers
last Saturday,
like a fluttering, floral tablecloth
tent-pegged to the ground.
By children?
Caterers?
Performance artists?
(Or is it a brick on each corner?

A shoe?)
The table beneath
spread with a feast.
You were the meal
piece-meal,
the excited bees'
jam, the hot flies'
lot. The cloth's
Egyptian history.

Do you see
pinprick stars
through it?

Or the smothering back
of flowers?

Calving Time

1
They arrive,
splay-legged.
September mornings
they are there,
new as this air
is to them.
They have rained
overnight,
parachuted in darkness,
have not been caught
in trees
or telegraph wires,
their gelatin legs withstand, dry,
their inebriate heads sway
and slowly right.

2
I find the dress
I wore to your funeral,
still unwashed.
It is strewn
with spring flowers,
it is torn behind one knee,
its hem hangs.
It caught on my dog's tooth
as I left him.

Its fabric too thin
for attachments,
too imbued
for mending.

3
The wet dress
hangs, flutters,
dries like a calf,
falls from its hanger,
dark red,
flowers;
lands like life,
deceptively dry,
viscose cool;
there is no feel of February.
It is undone cellulose, misspent calfskin.

Meredith Wattison's four books of poetry are *Psyche's Circus*, *Judith's Do*, *Fishwife* and *The Nihilist Line* (Five Islands, 2003).

John Mateer

The Gap of the Border

Tom Nicholson's Banner Marching Project

John Mateer's latest
books are *Semar's Cave:
an Indonesian Journal*
(FACP 2004) and the
poetry collection *The
Ancient Capital of
Images* (FACP 2005); his
art criticism appears
regularly in *Art Monthly
Australia.*

In Berlin, on one still but overcast day in October 2002, the Australian artist Tom Nicholson organised a small group of friends to join him in undertaking the initial actions of his *Banner Marching Project*. They gathered before dawn and were given instructions on the routes they were to follow and on how to bear the wooden frames which supported three-metre high banners of faces. To any onlooker, the band could easily have been mistaken for a political rally.

That the group of supporters was small and the message of the banners ambiguous – each of the banners used in the five marches only featured a generic face – would have made the cause appear obscure. Yet the nature of the march would have been immediately recognisable as a kind of political demonstration, though political in an elusive sense. Berlin is a city that more than anywhere else evokes memories of the Second World War, of the coming to power of Hitler, the advertising of the National Socialist Party, with its red banners of swastikas hanging from every building, and the ruins of Europe after Germany's defeat. It evokes as well the Cold War which divided the globe with an Iron Curtain. In this city images of the Cold War were those of *Die Mauer*/The Wall and Checkpoint Charlie and countless films featuring desperate escapes and spy-exchanges. For any bystander witnessing Nicholson's ambiguously political rally it might have appeared to be a reflection on political action itself, a meta-act, in that it possessed all the trappings of the political but without an objective.

In a city so overwritten by the process of history, so overwhelmed by the violence of its inscription and so punctuated by its vestiges, a gathering of banner-carrying marchers mostly following the course of the demolished Berlin Wall, walking sometimes up to their waist in long grass in what is now still the no-man's-land between the West and the East, and at other times toting the impersonal banner-faces into spaces where buildings once were, gaps in the architectural fabric, such a procession could have brought to mind previous political marches. If they weren't memories of the dramatic rallies of the pre-War years, they might have been mental images of other demonstrations, perhaps for Nuclear Disarmament or for NATO's intervention in Bosnia.

Yet anyone who considered the meaning of the portrait-images on the banners and who tried to reconcile them with the presence of the marchers or with the significance of the course of the paths along which the marchers were moving would have been left wondering at the work's strange blankness. Any inhabitant of Berlin, knowing the history of their city and understanding its symbolic significance and that of the Wall, might have presumed the procession was the work of an artist interested in 'making a statement' about the history of the twentieth century, a statement of the sort that has been made by many other artists. But more difficult to elucidate, as elusive and elliptical as the five walks themselves, would be the reason why an artist all the way from Melbourne, Australia, in the Antipodes, might be choosing to start his long-term *Banner Marching Project* in the German city. Any viewer would have to wonder why he chose to document these initial events under the title *Melancholia*.

Melancholia, that pre-psychological ailment of the mind, like nostalgia, is a word redolent of the poetic, of emotion and emotion's placement as mood. If the mood Berlin prompts in its inhabitants and visitors is something that an Australian artist can name as melancholia, it must be asked if nostalgia, its parallel ailment, that painful longing for home, is necessarily absent: *When melancholia becomes*

nostalgia, the sufferer's unhappiness may at least be given an object, a cause?
It was the strange conflation of melancholia and nostalgia that made
Wim Wenders' popular film *Wings of Desire* so convincingly and
movingly romantic, so powerfully evocative of Berlin prior to the
destruction of the Wall and the dismantling of Communism.

If melancholia is a suffering without apparent cause, transform-
ing the ailment into nostalgia may be a step towards recovery because
the latter, being an unhappiness prompted by displacement or recol-
lection, has a clear reason for its being.

In the case of Nicholson's banner-marches in Berlin, the melancholia could be the objectless depression of the post–Second World War
city, objectless because Nicholson was evoking the city before the collapse
of Communism and the rise of an economics of widespread consumerism
and its ideology of globalisation. The potential nostalgia that Nicholson's
work suggests for Berlin, his response to the elusive cause of its suffering,
its melancholia, would appear to be the subject of the work.

It would be easy to attribute the melancholia of the work, the
seemingly aimless wanderings of the banner-marchers and the im-
personality of the faces on their banners, to the city itself, to its
history and to that quality of its memory that ensures that melancholia stays melancholia and doesn't become nostalgia, a longing for the
Berlin of the past, for pre-War decadence or even fascist certainties.
The melancholia that Nicholson is rallying is that of the gap between
the full presence of the past and the full presence of today. It is the
lacuna of Berlin's history, that impersonal, silent smile of the unreal
– here it could be a Nazi face – and that of the split between the
historical past and the peaceful, Westernised, democratic,
consumerist present, that the artist brings to our awareness by means
of these meandering, banner-bearing walks through what was once
and, in a symbolic, memorial sense continues to be, borderland.

Beyond that there is in the mood of the actions themselves, not
in their necessary reference to the city, the suggestion of nostalgia, of a
memory of another time or another place.

It has now become common for art- and cultural-theorists to be of the
view that the public as a broad inclusive entity no longer exists, that

societies have been fragmented into smaller publics, communities that identify in complex ways, their individuals often making use of multiple identities and participation in various communities. Seen in that light, Nicholson's performance of the public act of political demonstration could have as its nostalgia a yearning for the experience of public life and for the activation of social meaning that that would entail, for the time when every member of a given society felt or – the Utopian view – *would* feel that they could 'make a difference'. This could be given substance were the viewer to know that during one of Nicholson's early investigations into public demonstrations he was given a photograph from the Australia of the 1930s which captured a Communist banner-march passing the Victoria Market in the centre of the city of Melbourne.

Were Nicholson's march viewed with this notion of nostalgia in mind, his undertaking the series of short banner-marches in Berlin could be understood as an ironic act, for wasn't Communism all about giving everyone equal rights and wasn't Red Square every year on May Day a paradigmatic banner-march? And what happened to the dream of the worldwide Fellowship of Man? There is another nostalgia implied in the banner-marches grouped under the name *Melancholia*, and that is to be found in the primacy of 'map-making' in the marches.

Intended to trace the urban and architectural gaps at the centre of Berlin, the paths followed in the marches were an iteration, a repeating of a Cold War demarcation, and were a confirmation of its substance. In effect, the marches were an illustration of that ideological division of the globe which took place after the Second World War and continued through the period of the Cold War and which has now been effaced by the expansion of globalisation and the unfolding of a new world war, the War on Terror, which has its symbolic origins not in the modern era but in an imaginary, medieval one.

It is in considering the relevance of this iteration, its relevance for an artist who grew up in the last years of the Cold War, who is from a country on the other side of the globe, that another, insightful nostalgia may be seen to have been produced by the melancholy Berlin banner-marchers. This nostalgia is not an iteration as it can't be a re-inscription on the site of an absence because its Antipodean longing hasn't been sufficiently declared. The nostalgia that Nicholson brings with him to the present-day Old World is the yearning for the reality of the past felt in the New World, the yearning to overcome the New World's seeming unreality and historylessness. The gap between the fullness of the past and the fullness of the present that Nicholson's work opens up is as geographical as it is temporal, suggesting that, in an important sense, the division between past and present that we presume is history doesn't necessarily exist in a New World country like Australia because, in a haunting sense, the country has no past. While it might be objected that this is a profoundly colonial attitude and is inherently absurd, anyone who ponders certain recent events in Australia – the ill-treatment of refugees, the denial of the genocidal intent of some colonial policies – must be led to seriously question Australian citizens' understanding of their own history.

Where Berlin, despite having been the focus of massive destruction and effacement during the Second World War and having the scar of the Wall running through it, is a city that has its aporia as gaps in the city-space, as silences in the ongoing conversation of its architecture, Australia, in contrast, is in its entirety – or was – regarded as a vacancy in itself. In the documentation of its colonisation it was declared to be empty land: *terra nullius*.

It is possible to see Nicholson's marking of the space remaining after the fall of the Berlin Wall as an enquiry after the nature of the absence that is the empty country, the no-man's-land of Australia. It was with *Melancholia* that Nicholson found a means of directly approaching the historical amnesia of Australian culture by identifying that inevitable hiatus formed in the process of making borders – that gap which is the boundary itself.

On his return to Australia from Europe in June 2003, Nicholson and his partner visited a friend who was working at Yuendemu in Central Australia. Having spent some time trying to find a way of staging banner-marches in Australia, but realising that the aporia that existed in Berlin – the corridor left by the destruction of the Wall and the gaps in the urban fabric left by the demolition of other buildings – had no equivalent in the urban landscape of Melbourne, Nicholson sensed that the Australian landscape itself is a vacancy, a gap. Thinking about the strange presence of the dried-up bed of the Todd River in the centre of Alice Springs, it occurred to him that there was another way of elucidating absence.

There Nicholson understood that the blankness which the Berlin banner-marches were implying, the gap of the border, the openness of that rift between the full past and the full present, could be inscribed on the Australian inner-city streetscape by reference to other borders. Any project to dramatise the politics of Australian blankness must refer to the politics of elsewhere – migrants to Australia are in the country due to the upheavals of the politics and economics of their countries of origin, and even the British settlement of the continent was a consequence of the complexity of European industrialisation and politicking.

Six months after visiting Central Australia, Nicholson arranged the first actions of the Banner Marching Project in Australia. Unlike the banner-marches which took place in Berlin, the Melbourne work consisted of seven marches that took place over seven consecutive days, from the 22nd until the 28th of February 2004. Announcing the marches in the Age newspaper on the day each was to take place with a small block advertisement, more as a way of recording the fact of their existence in the public realm of the newspaper than of attracting participants, Nicholson listed the time and place of gathering and an international border. The marchers who participated in the work had to meet at a prescribed place before dawn and, once marching, were directed in the course to follow, the course of the march being the outline of the border. On the last day the marchers walked the specified route without their banners, arriving at the art-space Ocular Lab in Melbourne's inner-northern suburbs to have a volkskueche, a shared meal eaten out on the street.

By following the line of a border which had been established elsewhere in the world during the twentieth century, a course super-imposed onto the streets of the densely inhabited city, the marchers were inscribing a dislocation. The dislocation reproduced was more than that usually manifested by demonstrations over an international issue – the people *here* championing the cause of Others *there* – because it was an iteration, an echoing, of the drawing of the borders. While the Berlin banner-marches were a confirmation of the actual site of a demolished border, the Melbourne marches were the assertion of the memory of borders and of the oblique and, by implication, often tenuous relationship that Australia has to them.

When Nicholson later exhibited documentation of these actions at Melbourne's Australian Centre for Contemporary Art in the show of new art called *NEW 04*, he included as a display, along with the large illustrations of the outlines of the borders and copies of the pages of the newspapers in which his block-announcements had appeared, an extended list of international borders established in the twentieth century, a list he had started compiling at the British Library during an extended stay in London.

Noticeable by its absence from the list, except for the first date, was Australia. Nicholson's open-ended chronology starts on the 1st of January 1901, the date of the Federation of Australia's States. The first international border he records was established three weeks later. At the time of writing, the list ends with the date of the establishment of the recent border between West and East Timor. While there were boundaries pertaining to Australia which he could have included, for example PNG, which was until 1975 administered by Australia, Nicholson excluded Australia in a manner that is suggestive, and arguably almost a provocative mimicking, of the popular self-conception of the country; that it is one territory and distant from the divisive international politics so important for the determining of boundaries elsewhere in the world.

Within the context of Australia and its contemporary art, Nicholson's decision to have the marchers follow the course of international borders would inevitably have brought to mind the difficult subject of the Aboriginal people's original ownership of the country, with all the mapping and politics that it implies. The marchers carrying the pictures of human faces through the dim morning streets of Melbourne's very nineteenth-century city, with its Victorian parks, terrace houses and trams, might have felt that they were, as they appeared to be to onlookers, like the early twentieth-century trade unionists who would march from outside Trades Hall into the city to stand, demonstrating, at the foot of the steps of Parliament House. But Nicholson's contemporary demonstration was of a different nature.

They, as non-indigenous Australians – presuming they were all Australians – were performing an act of double-inscription, one inscription conscious, the other unintended. With their feet, with each of the week's marches, they were marking the boundary of another place on the streets, paths and parks of this one, and in so doing were by implication resurrecting the nebulous sense of those earlier, Aboriginal boundaries which enabled the control of pre-colonial presence within this land. Nicholson's *Melbourne Banner Marches* are an appropriate response to the circumstances of a society that is struggling to articulate a sense of coherent cultural geography in the wake of the renewed understandings of Australian history prompted by the rise to prominence of Aboriginal painting, the exposé of *The Bringing Them Home Report* and the affirmation of the Mabo Decision, as well as by the political contradictions produced by the new, post-colonial form of exploitation known as globalisation.

That the banners borne by the marchers were portraits and that the marchers were walking the line of a boundary dividing countries distant from Australia from one another, their dissociation from the actuality of the place that is Melbourne and from the effects of its earliest politics, gave the actions, paradoxically, an air of indirection, and were for that less melancholy than the marches in Berlin, and more nostalgic. Spatially and architecturally Melbourne is more like the imperial capital of London than it is like any other Australian city, and because it has a strong history of labour politics, and is popularly known as the Australian locus of the Eight Hour Movement, thanks to which the eight-hour working day was established, the nostalgia implicit in the banner-marches which took place there, unlike those in Berlin, and the ones which were later enacted in the Western Australian wheat-belt town of Kellerberrin, could be taken as a hankering after another place, after 'a Mother England', and after the idealism of the best of its modern culture. The work's nostalgia may be seen as being for the time when international labour solidarity was a cherished hope.

For an artist to invoke the memory of a time prior to the re-structuring of politics by the process of globalisation with a quiet pre-dawn march is to introduce into the argument concerning art – today's argument about the power of the artwork as a form of representation versus the artwork as passive commodity – the awareness that the politics of the late nineteenth and early twentieth century, the politics of capital versus collectivity which underlies the entire history of the past century, is no longer an effective means of describing socio-economic issues. The faces which gazed down from above the heads of the marchers, down at the walls, streets and pedestrians of Melbourne in 2004 were as generic and deathly as the smiling faces of the social realist painting of the Soviet Union and of the pseudo–United Nations of Benetton's advertising campaigns. If globalisation has brought with it a single political misfortune it must be that it has collapsed the dialectic between Capitalism and Communism into a single, labyrinthine system of economic circulation.

Nicholson acknowledges that the iconicity of contemporary visual culture everywhere in the new globalised world operates on the sentiments of the individual in much the same way as Communist propaganda did – by the presentation of happiness in the form of the smiling face. Consequently the banner-marches are a critique of the use of the image, particularly the photographic image, in consumer culture. It is as if, by having the marchers move through the city bearing an image of a face, by labouring to transport an unidentifiable being's visage, they are collectively commemorating the demise of the Humanist individual, memorialising the death of The Individual.

When in October 2004 Nicholson took up an artist's residency at the IASKA, an international art space at Kellerberrin in rural Western Australia, he came to reconceive the manner in which the Banner Marching Project could assert its meanings.

IASKA is situated in a small town in the midst of wheat and sheep country several hundred kilometers from Perth. The landscape there is flat and relatively featureless. The architectural contexts that facilitated the meanings of the banner-marches in Berlin and Melbourne had no equivalents in a place where the town itself is modest and the surrounding country's most striking features are the Perth-Kalgoorlie water pipeline and the low granite-topped hill which gives the town its name. Nicholson used both features to direct part of the course of the two marches that took place there.

Watching the video images of the dawn and dusk marches of the 30th of October, the Kellerberrin banner-marches, in contrast to the actions in Berlin and Melbourne, seem neither melancholy nor nostalgic. Instead, they have a strange banality. The walkers, moving slowly with the large banners, first heading down from the rocky surface of Kellerberrin Hill, following the pipe-line, then entering the main street of the town, seem to be performing a task which is possessed of little profundity. The march is a spectacle of a minor kind. In light of this apparent banality, the ease with which any context for the events has been emptied, it would seem essential to ask the question of how the march's strange banality differs from the banality of the place and its everydayness. In looking up at the faces on the banners anyone in the street would also be peering up at the notion of the Person – that's in essence what every portrait is – in a countryside that is largely depopulated, twice depopulated: first by the 'displacement' of the Aboriginal people of the region, then by the introduction of industrialised farming and the shrinking of farming communities. Yet the faces are not ghostly because the context for a haunting has not yet been prepared.

Ultimately, the relaxed appearance of these marches affirms, despite its tendency to do otherwise, the complete pervasiveness of absence, the landscape's powerful historylessness. Unlike the marches in Berlin, which by their siting suggested political demonstrations, and unlike the marches in Melbourne, which evoked memories of militant trade unionism and, perhaps, pre–Second World War Communism, and even unlike Fremantle's annual Blessing of the Fleet, during which banners representing various Southern European communities are paraded through the streets of the port city before the fishing boats are blessed by religious figures, the *Kellerberrin Banner Marches* are an instance of dissociated social meaning. Where the Berlin marches could be taken to be a kind of meta-political act, a reflection on the idea of a political act, in Kellerberrin the marches become almost a forlorn gesture, an attempt to resurrect the idea of the social.

Although rural communities can be intensely social, often the more remote they are the more social, and focus around events like race day or the bush fire-service, they are generally conservative in their politics, and their means of asserting themselves politically by demonstrations very limited. Gathering the Kellerberrin community together to participate in the symbolic events of the marches, Nicholson endeavoured to situate a presentation of the Image within the rural, yet its outcome was the recognition of an empty, everyday Australia.

In contemplating the *Kellerberrin Banner Marches* it might be felt that the *Banner Project* has moved into a realm where the creation of historical meaning and the presentation of an image of The Individual is so tenuous as to be a mere curiosity and consequently banal. In Berlin the marches were akin to the unasked question – *What happened here?* – whereas the Melbourne marches, in marking their dislocation, their insistence on the spectral co-existence of the *here* and the *there*, with their outlines of foreign borders and with their resembling the early Modern demonstrations which politicised the exploited workforce, were an instantiation of the ghosts of the dream of the Fraternity of Man.

In Kellerberrin the marches became a non-symbolic wandering, a 'walkabout' enacted in a landscape from which visual evidence of pre-colonial culture has been almost entirely effaced. Nicholson's Kellerberrin actions didn't prompt the question *What happened here?* nor did it make the assertion that *We are here AND there*, rather it offered a puzzlement, the open, rhetorical question so many people ask themselves when trying to come to terms with the contradictions of Australia: *What is this place?*

Any answer to that question would be entirely dependant on the respondent's understanding of the nation's history. In the Western Australian wheat lands the politics that the *Banner Marching Project* implies is no longer that of even a notional contest between Capitalist individualism and Communist-inspired collective action since in that part of Australia those terms have little meaning, labour having already been replaced with machinery and its economy entirely determined by capital. The only politics of action that one is left to contemplate is whatever politics takes place in the distant city.

Floating down Massingham Street, Kellerberrin's main thoroughfare, it seemed that the faces on the banners appeared vaguely meaningful, like the portraits of dead relatives whose names were long ago forgotten.

Recently the Banner Marching Project has gone through a new stage in its evolution. The outline, Proposal for an Action with Banners and a Black Cube Hot-Air Balloon, presented jointly by Nicholson and the painter Raafat Ishak and exhibited in the large national survey show 2004: Australian Culture Now at the Ian Potter Gallery of Australian Art at Federation Square in Melbourne, is to conduct a future banner-march which will be accompanied by the flying of a purpose-built square balloon. At this point in time it is undecided whether the intention will be for the balloonists to attempt to follow the marchers or for the marchers to pursue the balloon, but Nicholson imagines it will involve what he calls 'a reciprocal following' as the balloon will definitely outpace the marchers, and the event will end with the separation of the two.

The subject of one painting in a series entitled *Variations and Corrections* (2004) by Ishak, this extension of the *Banner Marching Project* is an ingenious transformation of its thematics – the black cube, like Malevich's famous painting *Black Square*, the first version of which was painted in 1915, is a non-image, and will fly over the meta-politics of the banner marchers, scanning them from above as if it were the Eye of God. And there is another allusion, too, to the early days of photography, when in 1859 the Parisian photographer Gaspar-Felix Tournachon, popularly known as Nadar, was the first person to take images of his modern city from a purpose-built balloon and unknowingly set a precedent for the late twentieth century's technology of aerial surveying, whether that's the picturing of the earth as a marble-like blue sphere thanks to satellite technology, or the night-vision video images of missiles striking targets during the Gulf War, or the metaphorics of much commentary on Aboriginal desert painting which sees it as 'an aerial view'.

If the *Banner Marching Project* can be regarded as a critique of photography and the role it plays in simplifying the image: the marches present the banner-images to be viewed or photographed within the ambiguous context of the march, *Proposal for an Action with Banners and a Black Cube Hot-Air Balloon* is an advance on the logic of the larger banner project in that it accepts that such a basic understanding of the role of image-making in contemporary culture has now been undone by the technological innovations of new technologies such as digital photography, the Internet and the mobile phone. No longer is the image necessarily placed within a context of articulation or an actual physical situation. The image today, due to the transformation of the production and circulation of images, can't be iconic and can't be used to define a meaning because the site of its manifestation, its social matrix, is always in an excessive state of flux or virtuality.

By having the black cube balloon in the sky and the banner marchers parading on the ground Nicholson and Ishak are proposing that the conjunction of the contemporary image and the political is increasingly tenuous. That the balloon will be a minimalist cube, but lighter than air, and reminiscent of Malevich's *Black Square* with that work's implications for Modern art and its connotating of the Russian Orthodox icon tradition, the mood of this stage in the *Banner Marching Project* is also much different from that of the earlier marches.

Instead of the melancholia of the Berlin events, the nostalgia of the week of marches in Melbourne or the banality of the dawn and dusk rallies in Kellerberrin, the tone of the proposed banner and balloon march is almost tongue-in-cheek in a manner that indicates that it might not be inappropriate to view the coordination of the marchers, with their banners of over-large faces, and the black cube balloon drifting above, which is a singular, abstracted 'picture of God', as a parody of modern image-making, as a light-hearted demonstration that today's politics is no longer that of border-making, nor that of colonial and post-colonial distancing, nor that of the return to an emphasis on community and on art as a social event. Rather this future project might be something more moving and gentle: *Art as the Fanciful*.

Chris Andrews
Like Parra Says

Everyone loves to bag the individual
who happens to be inconvenient now
with an ad hoc category: women who make
slow hand gestures to display their burnished nails,
men who walk round with ties over their shoulders...
Maybe not everyone. Speaking for myself,
I hate people who say 'I hate people who...'
Like Parra says: I am the individual,
but somewhere in the world my spitting image
goes about his business and, creepier still,
my social doubles write something like this. It's
nice to have things in common, up to a point.
On the other hand, no one likes to be told

'You don't know what it's like', except on TV
where the would-be comforters usually have
more convincing comebacks than 'I'm left-handed,
I can extrapolate...' and the beautiful
suffer in your face. What about what it's like
to seize up when asked, Where do you see yourself
in five years' time? Or to have joined the legions
who have stopped smiling because of their bad teeth?

The Mist Lifts

The fickle insolidity of winter
in a higgledy-piggledy city full
of flimsy timber houses and brick veneer
(and stately Victoriana, to be fair)
as opposed to the monumental seasons
of Europe, solemnly inaugurated,
stretching forth like imperial esplanades,
or tropical humidity forever –
that's what we talk about over steaming cups
in low-fat sunlight. It has to be better
than perversely looking forward to the day
when life is finally brought to a standstill
by rigorously transparent procedures.

So this is how the mist lifts in a city
that some gifted children consider the pits
while others at the cutting edge of retro
throw a pinch of wishbone ash into the mix;
it lifts like this off a mirror-still river
where, as it is everywhere, cruelty is
unmistakeable as a triangle, but
midwinter's riddled with brilliant days like this.

Weather-proof

That was when the weather told you what to do:
take that book and read it on the fire escape;
the brick wall is warm and the wind is pouring
through a row of rain-washed poplars opposite.
You did it, but with a sense of loss then too.

That was when you were conscious of ignoring
the solemn imperatives of the weather
at your peril, but it's good not to forget
it was also when things you hadn't even
scratched the surface of seemed profoundly boring.

Certainty was watertight. You lay in bed
drifting imperceptibly towards despair
and still hoped you might find someone who'd tell you
about a trick for getting up proof against
the unpredictable weather in your head.

Chris Andrews teaches in the Department of French, Italian and Spanish
Studies at the University of Melbourne. He is the author of a collection of
poems, *Cut Lunch* (Ginninderra, 2002) and the translator of several novels by
contemporary Latin American writers, including Roberto Bolaño's *Distant
Star* (Harvill, 2004) and César Aira's *An Episode in the Life of a Landscape
Painter* (New Directions, 2006).

Lisa Jacobson
bathyscaphe

Five years it's been since Piccard* woke
to find his wife would not

and still the bed is polar cold,
his dreams snow-blind.

Most nights he sits beside the stove,
his feet fire-warm, and lets himself drop

down to the world that has no sun,
bathyscaphe groaning a symphony

till its touchdown on the deep-sea bed
where small crabs fidget on the ellipsis of memory.

And there he stays, as if in another galaxy,
witnessing the distant collision of stars

until birdsong hauls him up, too soon,
back to his chair, the fire gone cold,

incredulous as always that the clock's gold hands
measure something so intangible as ocean time,

which extends in all directions,
especially the past.

* Auguste Piccard: Swiss scientist and inventor of the bathyscaphe (1953),
the world's first self-propelled deep-sea diving submersible.

The Memory Wire

When I was twelve and in love with horses,
my best friend's dad sold fencing wire.
Circling the building where he worked
was a moat of paddock hemmed by fence
where my friend's chestnut mare grazed.
Sleek, long and lean, both girl and horse,
and hard to say which was more beautiful.

Then I knew the way that horses do,
when they crash their hard bulk all about,
that there'd be theft, and damage done.
Often a strange sorrow filled my hours.
This was in the days of childhood,
yet I was happy then.

Lisa Jacobson is completing a verse novel, *The Sunlit Zone*, as a PhD at La Trobe University. Her first book of poetry, *Hair & Skin & Teeth*, was published by Five Islands Press in 1995.

George Papaellinas

Waiting

George Papaellinas's
books include *Ikons*, a
collection of stories, and
No, a novel. He is
currently completing
The Trip, his next novel.

The one-year anniversary of the deluge that killed tens of thousands of people has just passed.

The *tsunami*'s been all over the newspaper, the radio, the TV…Everything. Talk about information-fatigue…

…I've had to learn an awful lot about fatigue lately. Too much, arguably. MS 'fatigues' me, you see. Not the usual end tiredness, but what they call *nerve* fatigue. A deep tiredness without any good explanation.

The media just loves going on about death. Much like its consumers do, of course. Its readers, watchers, listeners, whatever…

I've always loved reading. The newspaper, anything. And listening too. A kind of reading. TV, radio, whatever…They all involve words, anyway. Information in words…I used to read a lot once upon a time…Even if it was only a bad book. Something with gladiators, death or history.

MS is so full of ironies. I've got so much time now for the reading that I love. I've got all the time in the world. But one of the things MS has gone and done is blur up my eyesight…

Love might be something of an exaggeration…

Helen's the only thing I *love*, and she's not a thing, as she'll happily point out. Or angrily. She's a person. Go on. Just ask her. You don't have to take my word for anything.

The simple fact is I don't do books anymore. I do like leafing through the pages of my newspaper every morning. Slowly. It's similar enough to a book. It's a *faux* kind of book. They're cousins.

It'll never be the same, or even good enough. But luckily for me, I like listening too…Records. CDs. They're a *sort* of book. They're a *text*, as undergraduates are taught now.

Talking Books are the way my Helen's taught me to go. Bless her. She saved me from total boredom. She could see I was having more and more trouble seeing, reading a page in a book. The size of the print and blurry eyes before I'd even begun. It was her idea for me to try listening instead. I've listened to books that I could have once read. But not anymore. The first was *Lucky* by Alice Sebold, an extremely harrowing story of violent rape…I was quite prepared not to enjoy this experience, also as some sort of vote of preference for reading the book…I maintained my insistence on what I couldn't do anymore…I was harrumphing at the very idea of listening *rather than* reading…It was nostalgia for the printed page, I suppose. A rather sad, out of date one now.

Maybe all nostalgias are sad…I don't know. I don't want to think about it now…The fact is that I enjoyed listening to *Lucky*, in all its horror and pain. Sitting…back in time. Not that I would ever have had a story of rape read to me when I was a child…Not unless you count the fairytales.

Helen didn't stop encouraging my listening there. She read Margaret Atwood's *Penelopiad* aloud to me in bed at night. She read me asleep…It reminded me of being read to aloud when I was a child. Listening to a story being read out aloud was a curiously appropriate thing to be doing to a novel based on oral epics, influenced by the *Iliad* and the *Odyssey*, originally composed and sung to an audience by some wandering bard. Penelope's fate is curiously appropriate to my life too. She had to put up with sitting and waiting. She had no choice. She had to try and keep her hands and mind busy…Sewing and unravelling.

A little like writing and erasing…

Listening's not too bad a thing for a man to be practising doing anyway, Helen pointed out to me during some silly spat of ours or other...

I've actually got a bit of a history of listening. To songs mainly, that I've enjoyed. I pay most attention to the words, the lyrics, so it's a sort of literary experience. It's not a million miles away from reading books...

It's the same family, anyway. A kind of reading-fodder.

Though I must admit that I do more TV nowadays than either reading books or listening to CDs. It's the laziest option. The easiest, I mean. It makes things more real somehow. It's words too, don't worry again, *as well* as pictures. I've been seriously watching TV ever since I was a kid. It was on all the time in those days too. While mum got on with the cooking, the cleaning, cooking some more, the cleaning again, while my sister Helen and I got on with whatever was more important to us. We would've only just eaten, whatever the time was. This'd be a fair bet, given mum's interest in feeding her children. And then it'd be time for drawing, or homework, some reading, this book or that, or noising it up instead. Talking to each other, telling stories, which we'd do a lot. My family preferred noise as a background to silence.

TV's my good friend again. It's on all the time now, while Helen-my-love's out through the day. Working. Like the other few people left that I actually give two hoots about. Busy at their jobs, study, all sorts of things. I don't necessarily watch the TV when it's on. I just like its noise. It keeps me company, while I sit in a deep chair and use my laptop, or just wait and think. Or I listen to the occasional CD. And wonder big questions to myself, like 'Do other people worry about things as much as I do?' About rising water levels, factory emissions as thick as revenge, that sort of thing. People should be worrying. Australia *is* surrounded by ocean. It's *girt by sea*...

I've heard it said by Jungians, literateurs and hippies that water stands for emotion. As well as just water...

If it rained in real life as much as it does in books and movies, there'd be a *tsunami* every day.

I've only ever swum in the Pacific Ocean.

As far as Australia goes...I've swum a number of times in the

Aegean too. The Mediterranean. But we're concerned with oceans directly relevant to Australia here…Over volcanoes too, I suppose, under all that water.

Have you noticed how interested the media's become lately in volcanic eruptions? Vesuvius, Krakatoa. If it's ever erupted and killed people, then it's news. Or the subject of a documentary on TV.

I can't remember so much stuff ever having been on TV before about volcanoes erupting and causing huge, lethal tidal waves.

What a great word *Krakatoa* is! Like *tsunami*.

Words like these are pure poetry, whatever else they are. They *sound* great.

My sense of humour, my love of a joke, good *or* bad, my need to turn everything into a joke takes over sometimes and gets me into trouble, like some sort of funny monster. Eating me up.

There's a funny side to MS, as I always insist to my friends as they pick me up when I've fallen over *yet again*. But they never laugh. Even when I explain that I was just trying to head-butt a fly.

But I'm grateful for a sense of humour. I need one now.

My Helen's got a huge sense of humour…

I first found myself dwelling on volcanoes a while ago.

Well before I started thinking about their eruption and death. But it's the ensuing tidal wave that's really caught my attention. Helen's a veritable tidal wave of laughs herself sometimes. She cracks a joke and starts laughing, and it'll sweep me away.

My very good friend, Justin, comes over once a week now and takes me shopping at the supermarket, so I can contribute to the house a bit, so that Helen doesn't have to do everything all the time…

And I've noticed something…I've had no choice but to notice something, actually. I can't see properly in the supermarket. At first, I thought that this was because the supermarket's lit by rather massive overhead fluorescent lights and that this type of light disturbs my vision.

Then I remembered that a fluorescent reading light had been officially prescribed for me to read by. It's supposed to be *better* for my eyes. And it is! It works! So then I thought that maybe the reason

I couldn't see properly was ideological, that it's the massive *variety* of goods at the supermarket that offends me, the flagrant abundance in a world which includes so many poor, starving people. But, no. As Helen reminded me, the reason's much more prosaic. It seems that MS makes it very difficult to scan a large array of items and properly process the differences between them. It turns out that I'm even *neurally* offended by the excesses of late capitalism.

My childhood was good. Except for when it was bad. I remember Bondi very well...I seem to remember. Because one of the things MS has done is eroded my memory. I'd like to be back at Bondi now. Somewhere else anyway, some time else.

My family would all get down to Bondi Beach together once upon a time. Bondi's all of us in my memory, and not just me... A warm place. Especially in summer.

I used to get down to Bondi a lot. Dad's shop, the milk bar, the family milk bar, was just up the road. The proximity of the beach was one of the reasons he rented that shop. The old movie theatre just across the road was another. My dad saw huge potential in the milkshake and the lolly during intermissions. This location had a before, during and after too, he hoped.

Dad worked very hard.

There's a photo at home, a black-and-white photo, quite old, from back then, once upon a time, long ago, of dad in the shop, behind the counter, surrounded by his boxes of Clinkers, Marella Jubes, chewy things, and chocolate things. He's holding me up, his firm hands under my arms, to the camera. Showing off his boy. He's grinning so wide. He's proud of his shop, his boy, his future...

I take after *him*, apparently.

These days when I look into the mirror, I see my dad staring back.

I was never alone down at Bondi. At the beach, I was never lonely. There was always someone around, or close by, even if it was only everybody else on the beach. There was always something to do down there, and someone to do it with. Helen my sister, for instance. I don't think I can actually ever forget the wonder of the shallows and the little waves at the water's edge, it doesn't matter what MS does to me. The cold, cold at the edge of the sand. The worn, tiny, almost-see-through little shells there. The taste of *sea* on my fingers. The salt. The cold of the wet, if we weren't careful, the delight, the shock, the almost-tears, that'd be turning into pleasure soon, always. And my gran on the sand. My *yiayia*. Under her big umbrella, in her wet, stiff swimming costume in the sun. With my Aunt Mary, and my mum too, her sister. I've loved being down the beach, ever since I was a brown, little kid hanging onto *ma-ma*'s back, being thrown, Helen-my-sister too, into the bashing waves. Teaching us how to bodysurf.

It was my mum's body I first surfed, I remember, hanging onto her back. She's the one who first taught me what wet skin *smells* like. I think. Or my *yia-ya*, or my *nonni*, my Aunt Mary, mum's little sister. It was definitely mum's neck I'd grind my little snail thing into as she piggybacked me into the waves. I remember lying on my towel after-wards back on the sand too. Surf-slugged, sun-slugged, mum-slugged, Helen-my-sister-slugged, *yia-yia* and *nonni*-slugged too, everything and everyone-slugged…Yellow and blue are still my favourite colours.

One other thing I'll never forget, ever, from when I was little is my mother's leg.

The way she'd point her toe dramatically and tell us all a story. Me, my sister, my *yia-yia*, who'd heard it all before, and my *nonni*, who'd probably heard it all before too, or already knew it herself, and was enjoying repetition, a known thing, like we all do.

This particular day Mum was home early from work at the biscuit factory. And she was going on and on, as she would sometimes, about life in Cairo, Egypt, *back home* as she called it, amongst the toiling, well-colonised, brown masses. This was before she migrated to Australia, with *yia-yia* and *nonni*, when the man in their life, their protector, died suddenly. My anonymous, much loved and talked about grandfather, *pap-pou*. Grandad. *Yia-yia*'s husband, mum and *nonni*'s dad.

I don't know whether I would've liked him, or whether he would've liked me. I think so, though…

'Tents,' she'd sniggered out aloud. Darting and swinging her eyes between her sister, her mum, me, my sister. Her other surviving kid. As she remembered what the absurd, ignorant Australian locals imagined she had to wear back home. Overseas.

'Tents?...*Chanel*!' she corrected with a point of her toe and a wave of her hand.

Perhaps it's the presence of oral family stories throughout my childhood that has left me with such a strong drive to seek out story in whatever form I can, fiction or non-. Not that I'd ever dare to suggest to my mother that one of her stories is fiction...not entirely true.

But she was the first to teach me that the important thing when telling a story is sufficiently to 'persuade' a reader, a listener, a viewer, that a literal or metaphorical truth is being told. It's all a matter of technique. Authorial voice. That fiction and non-fiction are treated as somehow categorically different from each other has always struck me as ridiculous.

One of my favourite contemporary *fiction* writers has long been Jeanette Winterson, who often plays with historical reality. One of her narrators in some novel of hers or other, not all that different in voice to a non-fiction of hers, insists repeatedly that he or she is telling the truth, I can't remember which. Historical record would tell us that Winterson's narrator is definitely *not* telling the truth.

I've always preferred the truth as defined by Winterson in her fictions.

Mum was not a friend of the Arab masses in the old days...

Or the Aussie ones years later. Or any other ones. I'm not sure exactly where my politics...

In Australia, rich-in-ironies. My mum joined the working classes herself. She had no choice. My politics and my love of my mother now don't speak to each other. I made my choice between the two of them a long time ago. When I was little.

It was my mum who first taught me to just shut up and to like listening.

I can still remember my shoulders stinging brilliantly from the sun.

You can have *too much* sun nowadays. All that sun's not seen to be too good an idea now that skin cancer's *seen* to be the killer it is. But I remember those days very well, when there was still enough ozone in the air around us. Before there was such a thing as too much sun, and feeling sunburnt was still a brilliant feeling. I was a beach baby once. A real water baby. I can still remember my wet, long hair, when I was older, slap-slapping down my back. A sound as well as a feeling. I'll never forget my dad from those days either. He used to take me down the beach too, if he wasn't working in the shop just up the road from the beach, all the time, all the time.

There's strong evidence now that MS is exacerbated by a lack of Vitamin D, a lack of sunshine. What a choice. MS or skin cancer.

Though, of course, you *can* have both.

There was this other time.

It must've been one of my dad's rare days off. He's the one I remember down the beach, just me and him. I remember feeling vaguely suspicious. But looking back now, dad probably just wanted to bond with his boy a bit.

I can make things up sometimes now, apparently. Though I've always done that. But this isn't just my imagination. It's a brain thing.

Things are different now. Smells can happen, thoughts, and even people sometimes. I definitely remember dad though. He was in the water with me. We jumped up and down together, every time a wave hit, but really what I remember hardest about that day were the public changing rooms. I'd already been into the Women's with mum, when I was smaller. I could lose my breath in the Women's. It was full of girls. I couldn't stop looking at them, until I finally did. Because I had to. Mum was always big on decency. The Men's Changing Rooms turned out *basically* to be the same. There *were* differences though. There were more men in one, naturally, and more metal lockers too. And the showers were colder, if they worked at all. And the place was dirtier somehow. The skylights overhead were streaked with salt and grime.

But the thing I remember hardest is my father's cock...

His heavy cock was un-snipped, with a thick, big vein in it. The weight of it.

It was quite unlike my own more delicate, wounded little thing. Which still had a way to go, obviously. I'll never forget. It would all be mine one day.

Sometimes I can go volcanic. I explode.

Blow my stack. I lose my cool, or something. Out of frustration, I suppose.

I'll always have an excuse for bad behaviour now, at least...

MS makes one emotionally unstable, apparently. It gives you emotional *lability*. *Emotionally labile* is a nice way of describing someone who's *all-over-the-shop*.

I think about other things too, not just volcanoes...

It's actually better to be thinking about other things, I think, rather than just getting depressed.

I'm usually a grim sort of optimist. I'm a cheery enough soul.

I do dwell on death a lot, too much sometimes. I know, I know. Death by drowning, for instance...

I've always worried about drowning, all my life. It goes with the territory, so to speak, liking swimming so much, enjoying water so much, especially down the beach. Drowning would be an especially abysmal way to go.

People with MS drown one day, apparently. In their own saliva. They're unable to clear their throats...When I was still a kid, I used to duck my head under the water in the bath sometimes, to try and find out what drowning might feel like...And a couple of times down Bondi where I liked to hang out, whenever I wasn't home reading, I almost found out. I swam outside the flags, despite the obvious undertow. I overcame my panic, and made it back to shore.

I've got a Health Care Card now, so it's official.

I'm *officially* unwell.

I'm grateful, of course I am. I'm just saying. I'm grateful to the Australian people though, not their stingy government. To be getting my death-combatting drugs, paid for from the public purse, so I can afford them. And all my medical expenses. And a little money too, via Centrelink. The dole shop. A very little bit. It's enough...

There was this one time I remember. I was called into the dole shop, or disability support pensioner's waiting room rather, to enact the rather terminal transfer from unemployment benefits to a disability support pension. They wanted to see me in the flesh. In the *diseased* flesh. Helen drove me in and dropped me and drove off into the traffic. This was back in the days when I could still walk to the tram stop and wobble my way tiredly back home.

I took my seat in the waiting area. The big TV was on, too publicly I thought. There was no real opportunity just to watch and switch off. It *was* for everybody and there were certainly a lot of every-bodies there, so many people, so many citizens, that I actually began wondering whether Australian society might be collapsing. There were so many unhappy or frightened or angry people and so much noise.

'Youse all fuckin' molls!' exploded one *customer*. Though *client* is the correct description there now.

I'm not sure what his problem was. I couldn't even see who it was exactly. I did crane my head up and around, like everybody else in the waiting area did. But there were so many people around...All I caught a glimpse of was the security guard kindly escorting someone out into the street.

I heard my name called out. At last, I thought. I got up slowly and started making my way to where I thought my name had come from. I know I was very slow, because I do everything slowly now. I remember being slow even back then.

I was right. I found the chubby chappy who'd called my name. He was a frighteningly red-faced individual in a cardigan, as grey as some kind of uniform. He looked at me across his regulation, narrow, brown desk. Blowing out and puffing his flabby cheeks in annoyance.

I was already annoyed too. Feeling humiliated. He'd sat there like a lump watching me as I staggered and lurched on my stick towards him.

I sat down finally. Carefully. I can lose my balance, my equi-librium, if I lower myself too quickly into a much-needed sitting position.

I told you. I need my sense of humour.

'Why do you need a Disability Support Pension?...Tell us again?'

Because I'm an Australian citizen, and it's the Australian law, I wanted to say. You big puppy! And to remind him that he was a public servant. He worked for me!

But I didn't, thankfully.

'So what are you saying? You can't hold a job?' 'Not even fifteen hours a week?'

'I've got MS!' I cried out in response.

But anyway. I kept myself sitting upright in my plastic chair, I'm pleased, no proud, to say.

I remembered to keep my back stiff.

He shuffled through his papers. He found the form my good doctor had bothered to fill out...The brutally medical one that had asked whether I honestly had MS, whether I would ever get better, and whether this condition was terminal. Yes or No.

'We'll get back to you with our decision.' He'd just dismissed me.

I reckon I'd been waiting for about two hours, and I'd been at his desk for less than four minutes.

I levered myself up out of my chair, and slowly made my way out of Centrelink and into the street where I hailed a taxi and made it back home to where my Helen was waiting to laugh with me.

That office has been shut down now. In a cost-cutting exercise. And also, it was sitting on prime real estate.

Even so, I *am* grateful. Even to be alive...Even if sometimes I wonder. Why be alive? Just for the sake of sitting around waiting at Centrelink, or on the comfortable sofa at home listening to music. Or outside all my doctors' offices. At my neurologist's, my haematologist's, my psychiatrist's, my osteopath's, my pysiotherapist's, my occupational therapist's, my dietician's, my general practitioner's...

I'm native to Australia. I was born here and I'm the child of migrants too.

I hate to think what my life would be like if my parents had never migrated to Australia. Egypt, Cyprus, my mum, my dad. Countries better known for bus crashes and tennis players than benevolent health-care systems...

Things aren't singular or simple anymore. Complexity's the order of the day now. Complication. Compounds...Like the child Helen and I hope to be having one day soon. She won't be of Cypriot stock, or Scottish. She'll be *both*.

I remember leaving home when I was young. *Too* young, my mum felt. I'll never be able to forget her hanging onto my ankle in her desperation, and me kicking her away. Or dad's eyes. I'll never forget those either.

And I remember dad's smell.

From pressing my nose into his neck, when he used to take me in his arms and hug me. It's not a bad smell, a sweaty one, a working or after-working one rather.

There's one particular hug I'll always remember. That I can't forget. It was after I'd left home and I drove a mate's car over the gutter on the side of the street I'd moved to, and over the side into a rather rocky, abandoned, derelict lot. And caught the car there, the sump stuck on the gutter, scraping it badly if I tried to drive off. And I tried a lot of times, until I was almost in tears. I remember. And I gave up eventually. And just rang home, to speak to either one of my parents.

I spoke to mum, who could barely believe it was me, and passed me onto my barely believing dad. Who was torn between yelling at me in anger that I'd left home to be more independent and have fun, and upset my mum so, I could hear it in his voice, and relief and gladness. Which I could also hear in his voice, much to *my* relief. He listened to my story, paused only a moment, and reassured me that he'd be right there. And together we rocked the car, front and back, until it was free and I could drive it off, without another word. And I did. After just a mumbled thank-you and a hug.

And I remember the two of them opening the front door together, much to my surprise each time, when I finally started visiting them again, months later. Upright, proud and silent. Of course I remember. I can't quite believe my own cruelty now, but maybe I had no choice. I just had to get away…And where I moved was full of firsts for me. My first getting really drunk, my first proper, illegal artificial stimulant, my first big blue with a real estate agent, my first horrible neighbour, my first…real girlfriend…I'll never forget hanging drunkenly off a banister and dancing manically to a deafening stereo, to what wasn't, of course by then, my first loud rock music…

Granddaddy rock superstar, Neil Young's latest album, *Prairie Wind* is out now. I love it, thankfully. I've never been less able to deal with surprise. I can feel a deep anxiety…I'm not exactly happy about Neil Young's conservatism, but I love his music. And at least I'm old enough now to recognise that being a hippy, into the counter-culture, and being a deep conservative aren't necessarily contradictions.

But it's his previous CD, *Are You Passionate?* that I enjoyed much more frankly. And listened to harder. On one excellent track, dying's referred to as *going home*…Which makes it sound almost like a relief. Which getting home would certainly be when I was still a lonely kid too far up a road, a long way from where mum would be, already home from work at the car factory, already hard at work again, cleaning and baking those syrupy cakes I still love too much. Dad wouldn't be too far away then, home from the shop.

I've loved Neil Young's music, ever since I first saw him perform in the iconic *Woodstock* movie when I was younger. I was won. Forever, I suspect. For however long that is. I made the proverbial beeline for the iconoclastic *Harvest* album. It sounded so new. Tracks like 'Cinnamon Girl' capture the blissed-out, hopeful nature of being young in those days, with its belief in an inevitable redemption, what-ever one got up to, took or smoked.

Maybe that's what I'm good at now. Remembering. These records, CDs now, were the soundtrack to many parties, kisses and dancing.

When Krakatoa did blow finally, quite apart from the fact that hundreds of thousands of people would've been blown away or drowned in the subsequent tsunami, the sky as far away as Europe turned black overnight.

People must've thought that the darkness would be permanent…

Mary Shelley didn't despair though. Not anymore than usual, that is.

She just sat herself down, pulled out pen and paper, and wrote *Frankenstein*. She must've had monsters on the mind.

What she did is she wrote.

It's a lesson I should learn.

One of my all-time favourite songs, on CD now of course, 'Government Center', composed and sung by Jonathan Richman and his Modern Lovers. I first listened to it in a place by some water in Sydney.

I must have been stoned at the time, I think. It's possible for just about anything to sound good then, but I've listened to Richman's stuff countless times since without the benefit of a mind-altering substance, especially this song. And I still enjoy his work...

He tells me here, in this song, *that the secretaries down the Government Centre* need help to *feel better*. Having no choice but to perform such humdrum tasks all day as *putting the stamps on the letter, and then writing it down in the ledger...*

Richman is an extremely humane person. Yes, rock, rock, rock on, he exhorts, reminding me that even the dole shop's full of people, just like me, Unemployment Centre, Employment Centre, whatever Orwellian trick's being played with naming it Centrelink, now, a name that quite conspicuously explains and promises nothing.

Music soothes me nowadays...

I've been enjoying a great singer on CD lately, with a great name. And a great voice too. Kimya Dawson. I've been listening to her unfortunately-named, but quite brilliant album, *Hidden Vagenda*. On one of the tracks 'I will never forget', she insists that *i will never forget... i was so small/ wanted to grow in the eyes of my enemies/ for a while I felt tall/ but they knocked me back down/ now i'm here on my knees...*

That song saddens me, satisfyingly, so that all I can do is play it over, again and again.

As I finish writing this, I'm sitting quite comfortably.

I'm waiting in a plush vinyl armchair in the Oncology ward, a shunt in the major vein in my left arm.

I have to turn my eyes away as the shunt is being rather painlessly pushed into my vein. Expertly, I suppose. It's all *surprisingly* painless.

I usually expect the *worst*.

The shunt's for my regular infusion of a public health system-provided and administered drug, Mitoxantrone. This drug is more usually *enjoyed*, so to speak, by cancer-sufferers, but some researcher's discovered that this chemotherapy has a positive effect on MS-sufferers too.

First, my nurse, Jan, my *regular* nurse after three treatments now, takes a little of my blood.

I have to look away at this point, like I've already said. I know it's a straightforward, simple, *very* simple procedure, but I just can't stand the sight of blood...*especially* mine. The white cotton pillow set under my arm to help it not move while the Mitoxantrone's being infused, is suddenly spotted with blood. Just a bit. Which is probably from the specimen-taking needle, I realise later. My mate, Helen, who's come with me to keep me company, points it out, just before she changes the subject quickly. To something sillier and less likely to upset me, I suppose.

I'm filling my head up with useless words about useless anythings...I can just about *hear* myself doing it. I'll do anything not to think about the infusion needle. About the blood, or the just about crippling nausea I already know comes from taking the Mitoxantrone, and can expect now...

No!

I'm glad I took it. That it's available for me to take.

But it'll weaken me, you see, and I don't like it. It makes me feeble...Terribly. It frightens me and shocks me frankly, just how hard even getting down the hallway to the toilet becomes. I cannot exaggerate just how useless my arms and legs start to feel. Like I'm already trapped in my grave...

I can hear nurses joking with patients. The blue chemical's started dripping into my vein. Everyone here seems to have someone waiting with them, doing crosswords, reading books, talking to the social worker. Helen is sitting next to me, knitting.

We're all waiting...

Kristen Lang
completing a self-portrait

the sky's blue breaks through him; he finds
rain that won't fall, tangling in his fingers,
like vapour in the sun's glare –

   his cloud hands
         are clean
      with emptiness…

   And when he speaks,

he recounts how the slipped ends
of his own horizon
stretched him to the size of day,

   his tongue
      easing him
        back into the man he paints.

Kristen Lang lives in Sheffield, Tasmania, and has completed a PhD in
poetry at Deakin University. Her poetry has been published in Australian
journals and she has been awarded residencies at the Varuna Writers' House.

Tony Birch

The Good Howard

Tony Birch has published
fiction, poetry and
essays in a range of
journals within Australia
and internationally. His
novel, *Shadowboxing*
was published by Scribe
earlier in 2006. He
teaches in the Creative
Writing program at the
University of Melbourne.

A pattern soon set in. For several weeks I had been waking in the middle of the night. The first time it happened I was sure for a moment that I had wet the bed – a man of fifty. I looked over to my wife edged on the other side of the bed, before sitting up and palming the bedsheet and mattress. It was only when I felt my pyjama top clinging to my back that I realised it was sweat.

I was aware that I had been dreaming, although I could recall none of the details. My concern over the dream only increased my already heightened anxiety. Too embarrassed to confide in my wife I decided to talk to one of the other managers at the office. I soon realised this was a mistake. He told me that I should keep a pen and pad near the bedside, so that when I wake in the night I will be able to document the details of the dream before it vanishes.

I tried explaining my predicament. 'But I can't write it down. As soon as I know that I am awake, the dream, well, it has already slipped away. There is nothing left to write down. It is gone, all of it.'

He looked at me suspiciously. 'Well, if it's gone, how do you know you've been dreaming? You must be worried about something?' He put his feet up on the desk and began to laugh. 'Midlife crisis.

That's what it will be. I'd put money on it. He stood up and patted me roughly on the shoulder while winking at me. 'Don't let it get to you. Chat up one of the office girls. A night out on the town, that's what you need. You'll soon get over your worries then.'

I was stuck on one of his comments as I drove home from work that night – worried about something? I would not have thought so, not until he posed the question. But, yes, maybe I am. I must be. I am aware that in the minutes after I have awoken from the dream I have an overwhelming sense that something is very wrong, that something catastrophic is about to visit me. I just do not know what it is. And by the next morning, after I have finally drifted back to sleep, only to be shaken by my wife telling me that I will be late for work if I don't get up, I attempt to reassure myself that everything will be fine. It is only a dream, I tell myself.

But things are not fine. They do not get better. They become worse. The sweating and the nightmares, or what I think may be nightmares, continue until I am unable to sleep at all. I become exhausted. But then, strangely, just when I have resigned myself that I need professional help and will need to visit my doctor I sleep right through the night, like a baby, as they say.

When I wake in the morning after a full night's sleep I feel fresh and relaxed. It feels like a good day. Today will be my day, I attempt to convince myself in the shower that morning. The first day of my new habit, of sleeping through the night undisturbed, I tell myself. I have a quick breakfast, grab the car keys, and leave the house, deciding on an early start to the working day.

But the car refuses to turn over. I have a quick look under the bonnet before realising that I had left the lights on the night before. I go back into the house and tell my wife that I am catching the bus. She wants to call the RAVC there and then, but I tell her not to worry. There is no hurry. She can ring them during the morning. I am taking the bus, I tell her. She looks at me as if I am crazy. She repeats that she can call them for me. But I tell her no. Today it will be the bus.

Rather than walk to the end of our street and along the main road to the bus stop, a ten-minute walk, I cut through the lane behind the house to the nature reserve that follows a creek cutting through the middle of the suburb. I begin my walk along a bicycle path that meanders beneath a line of trees alongside the creek. The occasional jogger and cyclist pass me. It is a beautiful autumn morning, crisp and clear. I feel so happy that I begin to swing my briefcase through the air. I even consider whistling.

When I come to I am lying on my back. I can feel the familiar dampness of my shirt against my skin. I look up, not to the ceiling of my bedroom, but at a dappled blanket of sky. I try sitting up. I can see my briefcase between my legs. I feel dizzy and a little nauseous so I rest my head back on the wet ground and turn on my side as I vomit bile onto the grass.

A fluoro-suited cyclist passes me just as I am clumsily getting to my feet. She brakes, turns an arc off the side of the bike path and comes back to me.

'You okay? Can I help you?'

I look up at her. The woman is young, and pretty. She has straw pigtails protruding from each side of her helmet. She looks like a Viking. Viking Woman. I feel as if I am a little drunk. I want to laugh at her and tell her she looks silly. But I don't, because I realise that I am the one who must look silly as I have spit and vomit dribbling down my chin, the knees of my pants are covered in mud, and although I have not noticed it yet, I have damp autumn leaves stuck to the back of my suit jacket.

'Thank you, but I'm fine. I just tripped over on that tree branch, there.'

I search around on the ground, attempting to locate something, anything that may have been the cause of my fall. Her eyes follow mine, combing the ground with me.

She asks me again if I am all right before remounting the saddle, locking her plastic slippers into the pedals and taking off. I brush myself down as best I can, retrieve my briefcase and decide that although I am still a little uneasy on my feet I will continue to the bus stop. I have not taken more than a couple of steps before I feel a second spell of giddiness and then lucidly recall my mysterious dream for the first time.

In the dream I am in my house, which although eerily familiar, is not my house. I am running from room to room, becoming increasingly frantic as I open and shut each door. I get to the end of a long hallway, where I find an open doorway. I am welcomed into the room by a soft yellow light.

As I step through the doorway I see my mother standing in front of me. She is looking just as she did in the weeks before her death. She is wearing that floral housecoat that became her uniform; the one we teased her about because she was never out of it in the last months of her life.

The room she is standing in is not a room as such, but a long corridor vanishing into the distance. The walls of the corridor are lined with shelving from floor to ceiling. And cluttered along the shelves are the hundreds, if not thousands, of cheap ornaments my mother collected during her lifetime.

I look at my mother with fear, certain that I have seen a ghost. I then see myself, or my reflection at least, in an etched glass mirror on a shelf behind her left shoulder. But it is not the image of a fifty-year-old man I see. In the mirror I am a boy of ten again, with the head of blond hair and the soft unmarked face I wore back then.

I look away from the mirror and back to my mother. She has transformed herself. She is no longer a hunched eighty-five-year-old housebound pensioner, but a vivacious thirty-something woman. I look down and see that she is wearing a pair of red dancing shoes that she had favoured as a younger woman.

As I continue to the bus stop I replay the dream again and again, desperately wanting to make sense of it. I make a mental note that I will write down the details of the dream as soon as I am on the bus. While standing at the bus stop, looking down at my watch and then up at the timetable attached to the bus shelter I hear a voice behind me.

'The 8.05. The 8.05. He is two minutes late. He always is. He will be here in…in around ninety seconds.'

I turn around. I see a man, maybe a little younger than myself, sitting on the red brick front fence of a house. He has one of those old-fashioned haircuts that seem to have come out of the Great Depression; a razor sharp part down the centre of his head, a fringe flopping onto his forehead, with a shaved square back and sides. His clothing looks as if it comes from a similar age, although it is not aged or worn. He is wearing a checked shirt; buttoned to the neck, under a brown hand-knitted cardigan with wooden buttons, grey pants, and a pair of brown leather shoes, freshly polished.

He points to the timetable. 'The 8.05, it will be here in,' he looks down at his own watch, 'in sixty seconds.'

I do not answer him and walk to the other end of the bus shelter.

He is correct about the delayed bus. Before a minute had passed it turns into the street and pulls into the kerb.

My travelling companion motions me onto the bus in front of him. I look for an empty seat, at a safe distance from both the elderly passengers huddled together at the front of the bus and a group of raucous schoolkids bouncing across back seat.

As I search for a seat I can sense his presence. As he walks down the aisle behind me several passengers greet him.

'Good morning, Howard.'

'How are you today, Howard?'

'Lovely morning, isn't it, Howard.'

I take my seat. Although there are several empty seats on the bus he sits down next to me. He looks around and waves to people on the bus before turning to me, smiling and offering his hand.

'Good morning, I am Howard.'

I look down at his open hand before tentatively offering my own, although I do not give my name away. Howard looks closely at my face. 'You don't catch the bus, this bus. The 8.05. You don't catch the 8.05. What bus do you catch?'

I look ahead and answer without turning to him. 'No, I do not catch the bus. Never.'

He leans across the seat and picks something from the shoulder of my jacket. I move away with a slight jump. He shows me the leaf of a liquid amber. As he swirls the leaf between his fingertips the light picks up its bruised colours.

I ignore Howard and turn away. I do not want to talk to him, or anyone else on the bus. I open my briefcase, take out a client file, close the case and put the file on top. I take my fountain pen from my suit coat pocket and try concentrating on the paperwork. It is pointless as I continue to worry over the dream, quizzing myself as to what it may mean. I put the file away and take my note pad from the briefcase and begin writing.

Howard leaves me to myself for several bus stops. We pull in alongside the railway station. The noisy schoolkids from the back seat and a few other passengers get off the bus. I pray that Howard will be leaving also. But he doesn't. He appears to have settled in next to me. Some of the remaining passengers begin pointing to Howard and calling out to him.

'That's not you, Howard. You're the good Howard. That's not you, over there.'

I look up. They are all smiling at Howard, even the bus driver. He smiles back at them. He then nudges my arm and points to something outside the window of the bus. 'That's not me. I am the good Howard.'

I look out of the window but have no idea what he is talking about.

He points again. 'Look, that's not me. That's not me. I'm the good Howard.'

I finally realise what it is he is referring to. It is a piece of graffiti scrawled on the sidewall of the railway station – HOWARD LIED – AND SOLD OUT ON REFUGEES.

I don't get it. Not at first, at least. But when I do I laugh, to myself mostly, but just loud enough so that 'the good Howard' hears me. He leans across and smiles.

As we are about to take off the railway gates come down so that the train can pass. Several minutes after the train has left the station the gates have not lifted. The bells continue to ring. The gates are stuck. I rest my chin in my hand, place my forehead against the window and drift off for a moment. I feel myself falling back into the dream again, so I sit upright, wanting desperately to keep myself awake.

Howard leans across from his seat. 'Are you tired? You look tired.'

I try ignoring him but he won't be put off.

'You have to get your eight hours, your eight hours. Do you get your eight hours? You look tired.'

I look across at Howard, finally realising that I am stuck with him.

'No...Howard...I don't usually get my eight hours. I did last night, funnily enough, but most of the time, no, I don't get a great night's sleep.'

He rocks back and forward in his seat a couple of times. 'I do. Eight hours. Nine hours. Ten hours. Why don't you get yours?'

I look down at the notes that I have been scribbling on my pad. I look at Howard. He is patiently waiting for an answer from me. 'It's nothing. Just these dreams. I have dreams. They wake me sometimes.'

He becomes inquisitive. 'Dreams? You have dreams? What are you're dreams? Tell me about them.'

I look at him, this total stranger, who is probably a little strange as well. I peer out of the bus to the graffiti, and then back at Howard. The traffic is not moving. The driver gets on the microphone and suggests that the passengers may like to get off and take a detour via the next train. A few more passengers leave the bus. I cannot follow them, as I have to go across town. So I stay. And so does Howard, who continues to look at me, waiting for my response.

As I recount the details of the dream Howard appears to hang on every word. When I have stopped telling him about the dream I feel that my story is unfinished, that I need to say something more, although I am not sure what it is. I shrug my shoulders. 'I don't know what it means. One of my work colleagues, he tells me that dreams need to be interpreted. If we learn to understand our dreams, we come to understand ourselves. But I cannot understand much of my dream. Not just yet, anyway.'

Howard looks straight ahead without saying a word. I look down at the notepad on top of my briefcase while thinking about my mother. I feel reasonably certain that the dream must have something to do with her death. On the day of her funeral I could not stop crying. I was surprised by my reaction, although I should not have been. After all, this was my mother's death. But in the weeks before it was all over, when she had been quite ill and in pain, I had rationalised that she had lived a relatively good and long life, as they say. And that her death would bring her peace, as they also say.

As I had stood at the graveside my crying had become more audible. I looked around at the other mourners, a little embarrassed and covered my mouth with the back of my hand. My wife put an arm around my waist, attempting to console me. 'It's okay, it's okay.'

A few days later she commented again that it was all right to cry, before reminding me, 'You used to cry all the time when we were younger; at the movies, when Elsie had her paw caught in that rat trap down the back. You even cried when your football team lost that final by a point. Remember that. You were like a big kid?'

But I could not remember.

Howard pulls at my sleeve to get my attention.

'Tell me about the end again, the end of the dream.'

'The end?'

'About your mother, and the red shoes.'

I tell him again, about seeing myself in the mirror as a child, and then looking at my mother, suddenly much younger, all dressed up for a night on the boards.

Howard screws his face up while listening again to the end of my story. He looks down at his watch before replying to me. 'Your dream, I think it is about dancing. Your mum, she liked dancing?'

My mother loved dancing, when she was younger, at least. She and my father would go to the '50/50' dance every Sunday night at the Brunswick Town Hall. As I sat on the bus I could suddenly see them in the front room of my childhood home, ready to go out for the night. Him in black suit with his hair slicked back, my mother wearing those shoes.

Howard interrupts me. 'It's the dancing. I think you need to go dancing.'

I look across to Howard in bemusement, about to tell him that I have never been dancing, that I can't dance, when he suddenly jumps up from his seat and walks to the front of the bus. The driver opens the door and Howard moves to the lower step. He turns around and waves to the other passengers and then at me.

As he leaves the bus the few remaining passengers call out to him, 'Goodbye, Howard, see you tomorrow morning.'

Howard walks to the other side of the road and stands alongside the graffiti wall. The boom gates lift, which causes the elderly passengers at the front of the bus to cheer in childlike unison. As we take off I look over at Good Howard. He waves.

The following weekend I am down in the back garden turning over the compost. My wife is up in the kitchen going through the papers. I can hear music drifting onto the patio but cannot recognise what is playing. When I have finished my work I put the shovel and pick in the shed and walk up to the house, thinking about a cup of tea. I leave my boots and socks at the back door before opening it and walking into the kitchen. My wife is at the sink rinsing a wine glass.

I am also greeted by the voice of Ella Fitzgerald belting out her version of 'Mack the Knife'. As I walk through the kitchen, on my way to the bathroom to wash my hands my wife looks over her shoulder and smiles at me. I stop for a moment and look down at her hips as they sway with Ella. In the bathroom I stare into my unshaven and wrinkled face as the warm water and soap caress my hands. As I look down into the ivory sink and inspect my hands I realise that my bare feet have been shuffling an awkward rhythm across the floor tiles.

Adam Aitken
Translations from the Malay, 1930

Lesson 28: kena, to get or incur

The prau met with a stiff breeze yesterday. These steps were broken,
but I knew not why. For some reason I had lost my job, but the
writing room gets the afternoon sun, and the brushes get wet with
rain. My white shirt is ink stained, the arm of my coat is dirty with
whitewash, my trousers are splashed with mud. I live in a house of
wood that has been painted, and it will last for a long time. I got
Abdul to fetch two tins of kerosene and Baba had to pay the broker
two dollars commission. The cook complained that her knife was rust
eaten. Get rid of it with powder I said. Nonya had yet to return for
her mother was ill.

Lesson 29: Adverbs

I had heard enough. What else was there for the gardener had swept
almost everything. Eat some more, speak less, give the child more
pudding. I urged Baba to speak a little more quietly around the
guests. The driver wanted more wages, but how much more, he could
not say. Really! He is not one to describe things precisely, as he lives
in a world simply. The Sundanese maid is exceedingly pretty,
exceedingly. The cook's sauces are very delicious. So if you wait
awhile I will read all the letters. Please don't think I am an idiot,
James, well not completely. I sold the Humber for 100 pounds too
little. By the end of the month I shall be much better. The Padre
drinks far too much, but what's the harm in asking for a little more?

Lesson 30: Verb: boleh, to be able

Are you able to eat curry, Major? Or chilli sambal? I can manage it but Cook's never been able to understand that we Europeans can't take too many chillies. I can't believe you will be able to digest those kinds of vegetables! I usually eat cabbage in the morning and cauliflower in the evening. Cook's wife has learned to make ice kajang. Delicious, if the teeth can take all that syrup. A cigar? Yes, Driver might be able to take you to the godown. Can you come tomorrow night, Boy? We need an extra hand. (Really, Major, what can you do: if a boy's no good, it can't be helped.) Not much I can do to stop the milk going sour.

Lesson 41: Verb: jadi, to become

You must become a witness in this case, how the Sultan went to fat. At least Bun Keng's been promoted to master of the Hokkien School. It was fortunate for us that we didn't happen to go on leave to Kota Baru. What would have become of Baba? Worse Luck! the rain did not come and the wind rose. We wait in hope for the day when tapioca will be cheap. We almost went mad when the bangsal caught fire. Sometimes, I despair, that Boy will never come to anything!

Revision

What do you want to buy? A cartload of lime?

Go to the bank first and return by tram.

He seldom shoots of an afternoon.

How do you hope to be clever, Hashim, being always asleep?

Perhaps the padre will not return to dine this evening.

My, what a fool. He just does not know how to perform Boys Work!

It has been quite a while since he worked in a saw-mill.

I believe, all the same, he is innocent.

Adam Aitken teaches in the Department of Writing, University of Technology, Sydney. His latest poetry collection is *Impermanence.com* (Vagabond Press).

Fiona McGregor

Mutant Fiction – *Indelible Ink*

Work in Progress

Fiona McGregor's most recent novel *chemical palace* was shortlisted for the NSW Premier's Awards. In 2006 her performance 'duo senVoodoo' will tour to China and Poland.

Is it possible to imagine a story fully before it's written? Apparently Simenon did, then wrote it in two weeks. Sometimes – most often on the littoral between waking and sleeping – the story seems contained in your hands perfect as a globe. I luxuriate in those moments where everything seems possible. It's the seduction of the idea, the grand dream in which every absurd cut and scenario has a beautiful symmetry. Then you have to get up and start laying bricks with the shards of that broken reverie. I wish my methods were as straightforward as Simenon's, I wish writing was easier.

Talk about a work in progress must contain elements of bluff, quixotism and doubt – what you say you will write often doesn't eventuate. You can't be held to anything. There is something so fragile and elusive about an embryonic story – perhaps the materialisation of ideas is more of an uncovering than a building, the excavation of a ruin with a toothbrush – talking about it might smash your mysterious city before it's fully revealed. And how to hypothesise about the hidden treasure anyway? Writers tend to be superstitious because we are conjurors – we're terrified of jinxing our work before we've sung it out of the basket.

I began to write *Indelible Ink* as a short story in 2003. I had been working on the preparation for a big novel, I hadn't completed anything for two years and I was getting itchy. I had a basic story – an exciting enough event in itself as I usually begin with a mere image, place or feeling, sometimes the thumbnail sketch of a character – Marie King, a divorced mother of adult children from the North Shore proceeds to get her body extensively tattooed, then dies of cancer. Six months passed, I threw out a lot and kept refining, and decided I was really writing a novella. Another six months later, with not even a first draft completed, I hit a wall with the horrifying realisation that I might in fact have a novel on my hands. 'Horrifying' mainly because it still didn't feel like the novel I was *really supposed to be writing*. My little break had turned into another big project. I was unable to touch the manuscript for months.

There could be something analogous in Marie's compulsion – a small event leads to a massive life change, and she is embracing her fears to an extreme degree. The resultant exhilaration is what keeps her coming back for more: the site of fear becomes a site of triumph.

Likewise, I suspect a great deal of what draws me to this story is the opportunity to go against my past habits. I want to create a tight, plot-driven story. I want to write from the point of view of someone twenty years older than myself who has lived a different life to me. I want to explore motherhood in my fiction, unlikely ever to do so in actuality. I want to understand a woman who has subjugated her entire life to her husband and children. We are all products of our environment, whether generic or mutant, and the area that intrigues me most is the area of mutation.

My previous novel *chemical palace* was aleatoric, proceeding from flashpoint to flashpoint in an often circular fashion, driven by mood, phrasing, tone. Structurally, what it resembled the most was a DJ set – a series of seemingly separate pieces mixed across one another to form an emotional journey. It was, in the end, far more experimental than I had ever intended. *Indelible Ink* encourages me to go against all of that – it takes me back to basics. And the initial delusion that it would be easy was highly attractive to this doubt-riddled procrastinator.

But writing it is another story altogether. You're blind again, you don't know where you are, you stumble along sniffing out the next bit like a dog in the dark. I've been writing for twenty years and this leap into the unknown still shocks me like an icy sea. If it didn't, I probably wouldn't continue to write. I need this thrill, this threat.

Despite the fact that *Indelible Ink* is very different to *chemical palace*, my methods haven't changed that much. Initially I write whatever comes to mind – any scenario from the basic arc may beckon, and I pluck from the air the piece that calls loudest. It's like being on a vast plain surrounded by pieces of a jigsaw puzzle. I turn them over one by one. After a while I may be able to fit together a section. Here I have a corner, there a border, here I have a mass of detail that I'll put aside until I find a place for it. (Did another puzzle get mixed up in this box before I upended it? Are *all* the pieces really here?)

The first decent passages I wrote were the ones about tattooing. I was in familiar territory, and I had my first theme – the body.

The sessions began in the afternoon, the room in sunlight enormous around them, diminishing along the hours to a bright cone from the lamp Rhys positioned over the tattooed area. There it was, the expanse of skin from below her ribs to the top of her pubis, a canvas carefully, lovingly painted. Rhys a quiet worker, gliding on the wheels of her chair over to the bench to decant more ink and returning to Marie's side before Marie knew she had even left her. Then it began again, the searing cut, the drag of paper towel across the seepage, the cut, the drag, the whine of the iron, Rhys's smiling voice floating through. Hindu women were sometimes tattooed over the spleen and liver to avoid having stillborn children, y'know. Marie opened her eyes. Well, it's too late for me on that count, she muttered. Better late than never, said Rhys.

Marie was trying to visualise stomach ulcers. Did they resemble blisters on the epidermis? Spongy pustules filled with mucus? Or did the aqueous interior give them another structure altogether? She wondered how pliable they were, whether they resided in one spot like anemones suckered to the fleshy lining, or moved through the viscous bile of the abdominal cavity. She lamented her ignorance of the body. She sensed she must begin preparations for the hunt.

Now Rhys dipped a new set of needles into the base red, an alizarin blush that began near Marie's pubis. The next graze of paper stung her to lucidity. Marie was at once aware of every perforation, the stark tent of lamplight, the

tree outside deepening to silhouette, the mournful keening of Bulgarian
women through the radio. And in those moments of acute and conscious
pain when the interior burning surfaced like a shark fin through the ocean of
tattoo, she was stranded again. She closed her eyes and breathed. It hurts,
she murmured.

Marie lay there dozing through the final flames, the pain all around her a
hot red flood. She lived in pain, the swimming crimson of her eyelids, her
frantic pulse, the blood, the heat, my rose, a thorn, I'm burning, I'm burning.

Marie is completely isolated from any sort of body modification culture.
She's a 59 year-old woman cloistered in the monied North Shore. The
initial change she makes is as sudden and unforeseen to herself as it is to
those around her. Her first foray into a tattoo parlour is lubricated by
alcohol. She has an inchoate desire to do something completely different; to treat herself, and *test* herself. She wants to break out.

In less than a week Marie acquires three small tattoos. These are
cursory, reckless acts done in a parlour run by a man whose name she
doesn't even ask. She retreats, bewildered, to take stock of what she has
done. Her shame and fear are rampant, but the desire for another tattoo
is paramount so she sets out again with sober purpose and finds a tattoo
artist with whom she has empathy.

Rhys's works on Marie are creative collaborations, the tattooing
becomes an important ritual. Each tattoo is a sort of totem, a little
chapter she writes about herself on her skin, each is more sophisticated
than the last. She is initially too caught up in the whole process to care
about the social consequences. Her status as an aging divorcée was
already a step down the social scale; becoming a tattooed woman takes
her right off the ladder.

The shallowness of Marie's bourgeois peers is thrown into stark
relief by her new passion. This will be a rich vein to tap – nasty, funny,
satirical and dark. Marie will have other adventures once tattooed,
she'll embrace the whole notion of desecration. Rhys will be her Virgil
in the underworld. In order to succeed, *Indelible Ink* will have to be an
incisive portrait of the class whose taboos are breached by Marie's fall
from grace.

So when exactly did this mania begin?

Months ago. The flames were finished just before your dinner party.

God.

At the end of the expressway Susan took the corner hard. Pitching against the door, Marie imagined herself flying out onto the roadway, or better still, Susan beneath those screeching tyres. As they squealed up past the Conservatorium, Marie tried again.

I wanted to show you in private, so you could appreciate them.

Appreciate them! Susan's head swivelled. I don't think you need to undress right now, Marie.

For god's sake Susan. When did we become such prudes?

I'm not a prude! This isn't about sex!

I didn't say it was.

I-don't-like-tattoos! Susan's left hand struck the steering wheel with each word. You can never get rid of them, and people change.

Exactly.

Susan, who hated public transport as much as she hated the parking police, turned triumphantly into the one free space in front of the Art Gallery. Well here we are. It was meant to be.

Yes, said Marie affirmatively. I think it was.

I wasn't talking about *that*. Susan locked the car and went to the parking meter. With a long red fingernail she poked the bay number into the keyboard. Marvellous, there's an hour still payed for. That should do us.

Out of Susan's air-conditioned Audi, the heat wrapped around Marie like a woollen blanket. Her belly was churning. She began to sweat. Susan was looking up and down the street, one hand still on the meter as though steadying herself against a wind. Come on Susan. Don't be angry.

I'm not angry, she snapped. It's your funeral.

But I'm *happy* with them.

I can't talk about this now, Susan became flustered. I want to go and look at the art.

The queue to the blockbuster Renaissance show stretched all the way to the stairs. Susan stood to one side as though Marie were exuding a foul odour. You should put your jacket on, she counselled in a low voice. The air-conditioning's very strong in here. Marie ignored her, the tattoo barely visible between shirt and hairline. Inside the exhibition, Susan quickly disappeared.

A Catholic by upbringing and ancestry, but not belief, I've chosen an atheist context for Marie. It seems too easy to blame religion for our hang-ups about the body. Scratch the surface of many a leftist liberal, and you find the same prudishness, the same moral outrage about issues of the body that you find in the religious or political right. It's this deep-seated, universal conservatism that I want to attack.

Indelible Ink is about liberalism – not the specious sort spouted by safely waged middle-class columnists, but true radical freedom on all levels. It's about dancing with the devil, celebrating life in extremis, and going towards death with all guns blazing.

Reaction to Marie's cancer is coloured by judgment of her tattoos. I'm intrigued by the persistence of superstitious beliefs among the most rational of westerners – the common notion that the ill have somehow brought it upon themselves, that illness is a sort of curse, sometimes even a sign of moral delinquency.

There is probably no archetype considered as insipid as a well-to-do housewife – all the more interesting then to turn it upside down. Marie was once exactly the sort of woman that Howard's Australia sanctifies – a mother who stays at home to look after her children, the supportive wife of a successful businessman (her ex-husband runs an advertising agency). Yet in this guise she felt unfulfilled and worthless. In the guise of an outcast she finds strength, purpose and identity. And of course much pain.

What Marie loves about the tattooing is the painful process as much as the pictorial result. Perhaps this isn't so surprising, because a housewife's measuring sticks for corporeal pain include childbirth, just about the most extensively painful thing somebody can go through, and at the same time the most gratifying, and creative.

The seed of the more insidious pain of cancer is in Marie from the beginning. The expansion of imagery on her body counterpoints the metastasis of the tumour in her stomach. I want to play with the dichotomy of these two types of pain – the voluntary, transcendental, *rewarded* pain of a tattoo; the involuntary, terrifying pain of an illness whose prognosis is fatal. The tattoos are as much catharsis as celebration. Marie continues being tattooed until the bitter end.

I'm fascinated by the ethnography of tattooing. It's one of the most ancient and global of art forms yet so little has been written about it in terms of serious historical enquiry. The body arts have made a comeback over the past decades, but we still push them to the side and the current puritanical backlash encourages this. We trivialise them as we trivialise the body. Bad paintings don't compromise the Goyas and Arthur Boyds of our culture. Bad tattoos only reinforce all the old notions that the tattoo is vulgar.

The history of tattooing wends in and out of medical history to a surprising degree. 'The Iceman', discovered in the Otzal Alps in 1991, had 58 tattoos, mostly in the lumbar region and on his legs, on or near sites commonly used by acupuncturists to treat back and neck pain. His remarkably preserved body reveals that he had osteoarthritis as well as whipworm in the stomach. Otzi's tattoos were probably done to treat these conditions. Facial tattoos still seen among tribes in the Middle East are remedies for headache and sore eyes. Apotropaic tattoos were common among people from Borneo to the Arctic; ancient traditions are still extant among people like the Dayak. In western medicine radiotherapy treatment is mapped with tiny dot tattoos.

Often the only thing a writer has to tell them they are on the right track are synchronicities. The counterpoint of tattooing and sickness were all I had in the beginning. Discovering later that this meld has existed for millenia I take it as an affirmation.

I live in my books once they get under way. My characters drown out conversations in actual life and I transform from an engaged, reasonably gregarious person into an obtuse fool. I walk out of cafés without paying, I walk past people I've known for years without seeing them, let alone remembering their names. I leave the house without wallet, tickets, driver's licence. My vanity disappears. Once I came to in the bakery six blocks away realising I had a different shoe on each foot. Another time, in a main street, yesterday's knickers fell out the leg of the jeans I was wearing for the second day in a row. But even more ignominious is the mess in my brain, which I like to think I keep hidden most of the time. The most important questions in the world, the greatest dilemmas, are, What is se *doing*? And why? And how can I write it? Such selfishness!

Writers probably make lousy husbands and wives, but good lovers, preferably matched to someone with an equally foolish obsession. Marie's obsession is nothing if not novelistic. And in a sense, while I write this story, she is my lover.

My writing is largely driven by visceral engagement. I am Marie, with relish, under the inky needle, but to be Marie dying of a painful illness is an enormous challenge. It feels somehow a Faustian contract. Am I gawking at my own future death? Am I incanting some terrible prophecy? Since I began, three friends have fallen ill with cancer. Two have recovered, so their stories work as cheerful contradictions.

I'm probably just experiencing a typical fear of mortality. It seems more prevalent in our sterile, comfortable society than in others. The price we pay for our good health is a terrible ineptitude in dealing with death. A sick body fills us with fear and shame. I want to skewer this persistent Manichean split. Because we consider the body inferior to the mind, we often don't understand what a prison it is until we fall ill. Nor what a temple it can be until we decorate it.

Indelible Ink may be seen on the surface to be about the physical world alone. But like blood seeping out in the process of tattooing, the emotions, the psyche, the intelligence and soul of all matter bleed through when it is penetrated. As Rhys says to Marie's daughter – *It's not just about the body. The body contains everything else.*

The death of a mother is one of the most cataclysmic things a coherent family can experience and Marie's children began to clamour for attention quite early in the writing. None of them cope well with the tattoos – generational rebellion is flipped upside down. It feels apt as we watch a more conservative generation come of age. I'm interested in the pressure-cooker situation that Marie's metamorphosis creates for her children.

There is the eldest son, Clark, who is a Sydney historian, layering his sense of place. And I see these elements again – fear and shame – echoed in our history – then illumination in their embrace. He falls in love with a married woman, an illicit love that is inevitably shaped by his mother's death, as her death is by his love. Clark is a typical leftist intellectual, but utterly phobic when it comes to the body and illness. Visiting his mother in hospital is a journey into Hell.

Clark took his mother's script down to the hospital pharmacy. He had been here before. The long low-ceilinged corridors with their tracks of exposed red and blue wiring, the masonite walls. It was oppressive. He walked the downwards slope past an intern wearing a surgical bonnet, past a wide doorway, then around a corner. This was a new section, pristine white, fluoro lighting. Through a large window off to the right he glimpsed a walkway, a nurse hurrying across it to the adjacent building.

He turned and found himself back in an old section of crumbling plaster, worn lino and brickwork. Nobody around. He turned another corner. He was lost. Can somebody help me? The hospital seemed the perennial nightmare of this city of shifting sands, always being pulled down, always being rebuilt, every corridor sloping downwards, drawing him deeper into the bowels of the building.

Down he went, into the second circle, a sepia remnant of men cutting sandstone for the hospital foundations, and on through the Victorian days of carbolic soap and stout starched matrons and coppers boiling infection from tubercular sheets. Plague hospital, lunatic asylum, did they haunt the sick of today, those mournful faces of returned soldiers peering gauntly from between the sheets? The dead rose up around him. He went further, deeper, the thin backs of convicts flogged to the bone, the redcoats sweating, muskets loaded, the natives with bones pushed through septums and the staring women with keloid striations glinting in the sun. The air-conditioning hummed in his ears, the ducts like huge silver worms snaking overhead. What did they keep down here, what did they do? Perhaps around the next corner, he would stumble on a circle of figures stirring cauldrons of poison medicine. He passed two nurses wheeling a guerney, the patient sprouting tubes. He saw a sign to the pharmacy and followed it to the end of the corridor. At last! He handed the script across the counter. The nurse disappeared behind shelves then returned with two paper bags full of medication.

There is the middle daughter Blanche, ambitious and career-driven, in an unsatisfying marriage. Pregnant, freshly promoted, terrified of having another abortion, will she have to make the compromised choices she so despised in her mother? How important is a career? What in the end makes a life fulfilled? Of all the children, Blanche is possibly the most threatened by her mother's new friendship, and new life.

Why did she come here? Blanche said fiercely. Why did she do this?

Rhys paused, two cards in her hand. Because she wanted to, she replied.

Yes. And sometimes I want to commit homicide.

A small sound, half gasp half laugh, escaped Rhys's throat.

Blanche watched her warily. You don't like me, do you?

I don't know you. But I do like your mother. I love her, actually.

Love. The word inflamed her. Well why then, she said. *Why?*

I guess she wanted to do something for herself, on her own terms. She loved being tattooed. Every single design meant a lot to her. She could tell you better than I can.

Blanche hated her. Those mutilated hands and messy hair, her snotty-nosed brat like a bunch of twigs thrown into her lap, the black soles of his feet facing her like two shut doors. He was humming now, louder and louder. Do you just tattoo anything on anyone that walks in here? she said over the top of Travis. Take the money and mark them for life? Is that it?

Rhys drew in a breath. I tattoo consenting adults with designs that suit them.

Mum would have consented to anything after a drink or ten.

Rhys sat back and folded her arms. Nobody gets past our counter with so much as two beers under their belt. I've never once seen your mother drunk. She was – is – one of my best customers. If not *the* best.

I can see that. You must have made *thousands* from her. A real cash cow.

Travis slid off his mother's lap and crouched on the floor. He began to zoom his truck up and down with great crashing sound effects. Go upstairs darling, said Rhys. He left the room immediately and Rhys looked across at Blanche, her eyes glittering. I was going to give you the card of my acupuncturist –

More needles. Great!

Will you at least take this one? Rhys placed the second card before Blanche. All my details are there. I'll be out of range some of the time but I can pick up messages. Please let me know if anything goes wrong.

What more could go *wrong?*

There is the youngest son, Leon, a horticulturist in Brisbane. He comes home and cares for his mother's garden throughout her decline. He is gay in a homophobic family, and to have his outsider status overtaken by his mother, of all people, is at once disconcerting and humbling.

Marie's garden is one of the story's central motifs. A lush terraced slope threatened by drought, it is ultimately Marie's greatest achievement. It has a sort of immortality beyond all the characters, yet an acute ephemerality due not just to the drought, but to its impending loss through Marie's death and the sale of the house. So I return to the idea of indelible ink per se. Tattoos are for *life*. But a human life is so short.

The garden smelt happy. It smelt of death. Blood and bone, excrement, kelp and minerals from the ocean's underbelly, every bit of food that had been packed over its insatiable maw filtered up through the mulch and hung in a miasma across the entire half acre. She loved this smell of rot and growth, to be greeted on waking by the rank breath of her stirring garden. Early morning, she walked down past the banksia and kangaroo paw, past the euphorbias, lilly pilly and angophora, to the dank subtropical womb along the bottom fence. There, in the green dark, a new shoot on the cascade palm. She ran a finger along its seam and it unfurled like labia, the fronds fine and sharp as claws. A three-day flash of thick summer rain then the dry returned and the garden closed over once again. Muzzle of cicadas. Brown death creeping down the leaves.

There is a question emerging from this story – what is the difference between bearing witness and voyeurism? When is looking parasitic and when is it learning? How much empathy can we have? How much public imagery has economic determinants? – the political is nothing these days if not economic. The Kings are a television family, reared on the profits of advertising. Their cultural references are mostly audio-visual. I wonder how we are affected by images of catastrophe – I suspect we're not as inured to them as we so often complain. I wonder what kind of culture serves up graphic imagery of cosmetic surgery at prime time, postponing complex human dramas such as *Six Feet Under* until 10 p.m. And there's a perverse symmetry in the proliferation of medical and forensic dramas on prime time – once again, illness is at a remove, yet always before our eyes.

Clark revels in archival pictures of early twentieth-century Sydney crime scenes, especially the seamier stories of prostitution and convicts, yet is utterly threatened by his lover's past life as a sex worker, and titillated. For Blanche, a creative director in advertising, Marie commits more than anything an aesthetic offence. She treads on Leon's toes in a way he can barely articulate: tattoos are common visual aphrodisiacs in the gay world – the body art trend had a big impetus in queer subculture – but on a nice middle-class mother, tattoos are a heresy.

The older, tattooed lady is shunned socially, but tickles everyone's voyeurism. Nobody wants her to get another tattoo, everybody wants to see it.

And to what degree is the writer herself vicarious, and voyeuristic?

As imagistic as my writing has always been, I write mainly with my ears, constructing a narrative in a way similar to a musician constructing a piece of music. Each character is like an instrument, their interactions creating particular discords and harmonies. Each character has his or her idiosyncratic range and tone. In the final drafts of a story, I begin to hear where someone should come in more clearly, I literally finetune.

What remains consistent in my work and, I hope, grows stronger, is spirit of place. I can't imagine writing about much besides Sydney ever again. This ravaged, ravishing, mercurial city is my real main character. Sydney is the essence I'm always trying to capture. And the fear and shame are there again, of not measuring up to my material. But the desire to embrace and overcome them is stronger.

And what better setting for a book concerned with the transient nature of life? Sydney is literally built on sand, it's an architectural joke for the most part. Encircled by ocean, mountains and bush, Sydney is one of those cities you can imagine sinking back into the landscape within years of being ruined. And it is constantly being ruined.

So I've built myself a suburban sprawl, but I would be just as happy if *Indelible Ink* could be distilled back to a high-density novella or short story. At this stage it seems unlikely. But anything can happen in fiction.

Jean Kent

A Luminous Tortoise Near Muswellbrook

Approaching Muswellbrook, a city with a name promising
sinuous organisms
in a watery expanse the early settlers must have brought
whole, in their minds, from England

suddenly on the bitumen I see this tortured rag –
an old cardigan perhaps, one black arm flung out –

The car glides clean above it. By good fortune and speed
rather than my careful manoeuvring,
no damage is done…
It's the sound of expiry in the seat beside me, the balloon-loss
of your breath

that sharpens my sight in hind-sight –

brings me back from a dream of words
so that I see, too late, almost

                    yes, it *was* a tortoise,
a poured dark slick of animal life, following its risky neck
across the pelting highway.

Behind us are open cut mines, pits of lead-grey waste,
chimneys which from a distance
look like the hooves

of giant mules, cast-off carapaces sweltering up
time turned toxic –

From our still point as we pass, we read the contradicting
signs, say *steam steam* and try to believe...

As now I try to believe it's still there, too – that chug in the mind
of muscles and flesh under an unpromising shell,
that wave in the void like a poem
sticking its neck out:

this tortoise, luminous in my rear-vision lake.

Jean Kent lives at Lake Macquarie, NSW. She has published three
collections of poetry. Her most recent book, *The Satin Bowerbird* (Hale &
Iremonger), won the 1998 Wesley Michel Wright Prize.

Don Diespecker

Lightly Falling

Don Diespecker lives on the banks of the Bellinger River. He writes novels, essays, verse, caprice and military history. Two of his novellas were published as *The Agreement* by Homosapien Books in 2004.

The old man sat comfortably in the garden seeing leaves falling from the white cedars. Earlier he'd been certain that it was a good time to be writing, but, he now realised, time for seeing was equally important, perhaps more so. One wrote about realities of one kind or another. Many writings began as imagery that wavered into movement or dialogue and triggered an abundance of jostling ideas. Favourite characters from the current work in progress, not wanting to miss anything, would hijack their unsubtle ways into *his* images, urging dialogues and interior monologues. Other, more controllable, writings began with anything and everything that could be seen in the natural world: like the yellow cedar leaves falling, so many of them letting go almost at the same time. What if he thought of them as *golden* leaves, what then? 'Gold' might simply be an anthropocentric indulgence, a gloss, but so might 'yellow' be. Perhaps in Nature, trees simply allowed parts of themselves to fall away, and always lightly.

That was one of the good things about himself, he decided: he accepted all awareness without demur and generally with a smile, lightly. However painful it might sometimes be, awareness was always worth its weight in gold. 'By gold love is procured,' he whispered, remembering Ovid's writing of the golden age, about the highest honour coming from gold. And everything changes, he knew.

He could see gold spread generously in views through the garden and along the river and on the forested slopes. He recalled images of gold in paintings he had seen. He thought of ultra thin gold leaf, aptly named, fluttering when lifted by tweezers. The gold leaf used by artists and decorators seemed to him to indeed be leaf-light when he thought on it. It fluttered flimsily. Gold of a similar sheen had a delicate lightness when seen late in the afternoon on the surface of the river, downstream. The reflected colours of the hillside forest, made when the setting sun blazed eastward to cover the trees, added an extra glow that produced a patina of soft reflected light on the water. Afternoons at the end of February were like that: soft, subtle and delicate. When he sat outside at the garden's edge, close to the river bank, he was the privileged spectator, seeing downriver in a world of green and gold. But that wasn't it, not entirely, anyway. It was some-thing seen from inside the house while looking out through any of the many windows: leaves falling. There were songs about that, songs from the 1930s, for instance, love songs composed of loving images.

He remembered the falling leaves at Easter. He'd noticed them in the preceding days of an Indian summer abruptly changing to damp and rainy days; and with some days being so cool in the early mornings that he'd several times guessed: fourteen degrees or so, maybe fifteen. Following the falling-full-ness of the temperature, through his mind's eye, he saw himself coming carefully downstairs into the big lounge room overlooking a chilly-looking and misted river and imagining flames before the slow combustion heater enlivened. Sometimes in winter even seventeen seemed low enough to light the fire. He felt the cold the older he got. It could probably be graphed. He was generally accurate in guessing ahead at the temperature and smiled when the thermometer on his writing table confirmed his prediction. Did the aged become exquisitely sensitive to temperature changes? He'd begun doing aged things: keeping a fire going inside the house, keeping the blood moving warmly, if not hotly. Fires required preparation and decent wood mixed with lesser, dampish, windfall pieces; a reasonable wood fire to burn readily and throw out warmth. His mind peacefully remembered the image of finding a long, heavy, twisted dead branch fallen from one of the older *grandis* trees the previous afternoon: one of the most handsome of flooded gums had dropped a damaging branch, a widow-maker if ever there was one. Perhaps after years of dying gracefully it was unwanted by the tree. It came down heavily. He'd had his eye on it for several years. It was so long, so ungainly and straggly, but the base end was thick and heavy. When it comes down, he'd often thought, it'd cause some damage, even from that modest height. It had only to fall ten metres or so, and of course it did, and further wrecked a grapefruit tree whose trunk remained partly buried, almost half buried, in the flood loam dumped by the March 2001 floods. Ripening fruits from the stricken tree were now scattered on the grass and *lightly falling* wasn't fitting: the limb crashed down heavily but then was instantly firewood, quite decent firewood, hard and dry and demanding some axe work, even some sawing, and his neck no doubt jerked painfully out of harmony again, but he'd balance that cost with the getting of good wood.

And then the Indian summer had returned, and so it was warm and sunny again. The falling branch hadn't struck what was left of the hail-damaged dahlias and the colours were splendid, especially the dark reds and the pale blues, one a colour that was perhaps violet or a light purple. Perhaps he suffered from an anomalous colour defect. That was something else to look into. The dahlias had made a good recovery, a great show after the hail, easily putting out masses of colour from the wrecked foliage. Stricken plants were good at healing themselves. Lightly, easily as plants were wont to do. There was the temptation to sit outside with a glass of Shiraz and a book, a clipboard and pens, and even to sit in a well-lighted softly sunny patch, except that in those autumn days the best riverside sunny patches were invariably beneath the high stretched-out and strong (but increasingly aged) limbs of a particular white cedar, a tree that'd overseen many floods, had tolerated fishing eagles landing bouncingly on its dead branches and sometimes breaking them off, and was the friendly old host, or probably hostess, to endless feeding parties of brown fruit pigeons and sometimes too of booming *wompoo* pigeons, every autumn. The pigeons had a taste for the hanging bunches of golden seeds that glowed attractively at the filigree ends of leafless branches and branchlets when autumn was turning to winter. The pigeons hung at all angles and fed, immune to the poisonous flesh that humans couldn't tolerate. Loose ripe berries pattered down and disappeared into the undergrowth of the river bank like hopelessly lost small change. He often sat and watched at lunchtime, when the sun was high and the sky like bright blue parchment, seeing gold falling from heaven. In the late summer there was still some foliage on the ends of branchlets, the seeds like little hard green bullets, ripening slowly toward golden softness for the pigeon forays. He sat there in all weathers and in all seasons, and occasionally into the darkness of early evening when it was warm or mild, because it was always a remarkable place to sit and to see what could be seen. It'd almost always been a matter of the light and of the lighted afternoons, especially those late February afternoons, the soft green and gold scene that he could conjure up at any time wherever he happened to be, the glowing watercolour look of the Bellinger downstream, directly in front of where he sat, seeing along a personal line of sight. He'd quietly hinted to the hidden painter within that he would, one day, attempt to paint the scene, yet never had. It was for seeing, perhaps: he'd only to receive it like a gift, an epiphany of long afternoon moments, the surface of the river magically conveying itself to him.

In the Easter-time Indian summer of 2004, with his clipboard and pens, a book or two and a drink, he'd sought a safe place that was well lighted and not too hot. The dappled shade of the early afternoon wasn't only increasingly damp, it was continuously and boldly occupied as a forward base by squadrons of midges coming in from the Deep Shade, attracted by the human target, and they invariably made such randomly lighted places chiaroscuro killing grounds: landing softly, drilling lightly, sucking silently. He'd imagined with some foreboding that if he sat there long enough he'd be utterly drained by the elegant winged hordes and his dried-out remains, as light as dust motes, would be wafted away on slight breezes, possibly high and balmy breezes, so that the bits of him that once mattered, now airy husks, would float about somewhere above the shimmering river, somewhere between Heaven and Earth. It was a sobering thought, so sobering that he felt compelled to stand from time to time and wander about admiring the reborn colourful dahlias and pausing to bend down and say a few words to his favourite water dragon, who unblinkingly tolerated his eccentricity. Dragons liked fat stinging flies. Humans were mere stalking horses for dragons. Death by voracious midges seemed an unnecessarily serious thought and sunny afternoons were better devoted to being fully present, he knew. Sitting down again was like a fresh start. Head back he'd stare anew into the canopy of the dangerous old cedar. Bits had fallen off over the years: twenty years in *his* experience, to be exact, and probably more years than that when there was nobody in the same space to have experienced such events. Storms had wrecked the once-beautiful symmetry of the high branches. Falling branches had always missed him, fortuitously; tiny twigs came safely down silently and rapped one about the head or shoulders. A branch only millimetres thick and falling from a great height would certainly penetrate the best of skulls and a big, heavy branch would kill; no doubt about it, even if it could be heard coming noisily. He sometimes imagined it: the fumbled attempt to put down his wine (or shockingly: to hurl it aside), the lurching heave to achieve some form of crouching scramble, books and papers flying, and the attempt almost certainly failing because gravity compelled heavy things downward faster than he could leap upward. He remembered the time when a tree fell on the house and he was in the smallest room, hearing the gunshot cracks, knowing it would hit him if he moved. He stayed put. He had been right, for once.

In the clear autumn light he also continued to see two kinds of butterflies in the garden. Perhaps they were confident of its still being summer. One was medium-sized and mostly black and white; the others were small, and although pale yellow, nothing like the bigger yellow butterflies swooping and darting so speedily in the February-hot gardens, not those ones. These little fellows were yellow bobbers. Here it was April and already a third of it gone. *Lightly falling*: he frowned momentarily to think that *lightly landing* was just as significant, but it hardly mattered. For he'd seen several times through various windows, from inside the downstairs lounge room or upstairs through the higher windows, parties of leaves falling, hurrying down collectively to take their assigned places on the ground: small yellow to golden and some more faded leaves coming down in twisting clusters from the high branches of the white cedars, fluttering and shining in the sunlight and that was just fine and it was certainly beautiful, flagging the approaching completion of autumn, and what puzzled him immensely, was why the leaves came tumbling down in unison even when there was no wind blowing, no breeze, not the slightest moving of air that he could see and, when he checked, there were hardly ever fruit pigeons rambling about the high branches. The leaves had to be falling, moved either momentously by an invisible Heaven's Breath, or by some awful occult event beyond his comprehension. The lovely coloured leaves always fluttered as casually as snowflakes, like golden snow in flurries, seemingly random, yet that surely was not random, nor casual. It was as if the leaves were sent forth by parental decision: it's time to go, young'uns. Let go and fly away down. It was something like that, perhaps, and of course it wasn't only the white cedars that arranged these terminal embarkation flights: the flooded gums, the magnificently tall and straight eucalypts, did it too but not always at the same times. The gum leaves fell to the beat of a different baton, yet were also orchestrated to descend together, just like the cedar leaves. It couldn't be said that the leaves, of any tree, of any species, decided when to fall: the trees made the decisions. Yet the leaves knew when it was time to let go, however well connected they'd been, and to fall. Life was filled with obvious mysteries, yet airy explanations were always forthcoming. For lightness was everywhere. All of autumn was light and golden, because of the drought, except on rare grey and rainy days; then the world sank heavily under a universal blanket of wet air weighing on trees, on leaves, and the lightest of tiny flying creatures were grounded. Damp air generally suited big birds like cormorants that used it sensibly. Cormorants would fly in, often coming down steeply over the road bridge and then landing downstream, going with the flow, and always faultlessly, braking against the cushioning, denser air with feet splayed and the water spraying out and their broad black wings slowing them to perfection, to a skidding sliding stop exactly where they planned to be. They were a delight to see taking off too, beating strongly while still in the river, rising powerfully up, lifting directly into the air. He marvelled at the energy needed to do that. Then often to head upstream, beating up over the wet air above the rapids where the torrents ran into Champagne Pool, and over the bridge again deftly, their rates of climb perfectly judged. What artistry! Such aerial skills! Humans needed painstakingly to learn the extraordinary lessons of flying aircraft, aided by elaborate instrumentation. Birds did it naturally. Humans sometimes flew machines into obstacles like bridges and mountains and trees that could be seen. Birds hit only misperceived windows.

There were many smaller birds, almost always. The showiest were white-eared flycatchers: they owned the weeping coral tree close to the old birdbath and jumped out demonstratively to let him know they meant business: the birdbath was *also* theirs. They adapted some of their flying and hunting skills so that they tumbled in an airspace of less than half a metre, in and out of the water splashing, doing graceful half swoops and bobs, constantly moving, every movement meticulous or artistic. Very showy! A pleasure to see: could they be *entertaining* the grounded slumped human? Hardly. Why would they? All the birds were accomplished in their movements. Robins would bounce *up* the rough vertical trunks of old bloodwoods, effortlessly, without ever putting a claw wrong, without ever staggering or reeling or falling off. That was surely the equivalent of a human climber throwing himself freely upwards from a rock face, and then landing with complete and gripping confidence higher up: new fingerholds, new toeholds, as if by magic. And then there were the ants, one particular species that had, for at least twenty years, gone up and down the creamy grey trunk of a very high old flooded gum near the river bank. They went straight up in never-ending columns, came down the same way, streams of them, droves of them. Did they live up there, or down here? Why did they do it? The tree height in ant terms was higher than the highest of skyscrapers: the ants moved steadily, even hurriedly sometimes, and *vertically*. What if it were a game, an exhibitionistic game, for the ants? What if they went as high as they could to see the greater world: the river rolling down, its surface shiny and swirling, the endless forests, the changing lights of each day? What if a few of them threw themselves off to float down through the buoyant air, like autumn leaves, falling? Might ants do that, some types of ants?

In the garden during the warmer Easter days and in the moving patches of light that he had to keep moving from doubtfully, and sometimes abandoning, and sometimes satisfactorily manoeuvring further into, while the sun swung across the blue sky, he came to within two metres of the shaded birdbath. He looked over his glasses, over his book or papers or glass, and smiled, and the birds accepted his largely motionless presence. The birds always hopped in from the rim in a sprightly fashion, whatever the breed or species, some of them keeping an eye on the benign rural human. Perhaps they sensed he lacked the will to catch or to kill them.

After the bird show he walked slowly up to the house, still aware of the late afternoon sights and sounds, relishing being in the bigger system, not quite wanting to leave it for anything different or confining. Yet there were so many windows to see through that from within the house it was almost like being outside. The day had been good to him and very good for him, he reflected. Writings were written. Repose was granted him in the riverside gardens. He was privileged and could feel the sensation of privilege almost tingling upward through him. He went upstairs, still enamoured of the magical views through the dusty windows, and on the top step, turning, he suddenly became aware again of a familiar scene, a scene of scenes, that could often be viewed in afternoons of good light: varied images on tree trunks, and distantly *projected* blurred images of birds on nearby tree trunks. In the mellow light of the setting sun, when only the higher parts of the flooded gum trunks still had a glowing soft light on them, ten to twenty metres up, were the soft and fuzzy images of birds cast from other, sometimes distant, branches between the setting sun and the garden trees, their projected forms moving lightly on the vertical screens of cream and white tree trunks. Silent movies, soft light pictures, delicately moving avian actors in their own picture show, light images like living totems. Was he the entire audience? Could the birds see what he could see? Perhaps they could see their own shadow-graphs? Were the gardens a kind of theatre?

He continued seeing what could be seen until the last of the sun's light faded away and although he could no longer see the images falling on the tree trunks he continued to hear the birdsongs for long minutes.

Like curtain calls, like encores.

Cath Kenneally

Head floating in mid-air, an aura surrounds
you as you step, new-minted, into the garden, where
greens ambush you, sharp, citric nibs of Geraldton Wax,
spearlets, yellower green, of bamboo, comforting
blue-green of gum leaves, dark moss-green creeper
fronds, tough all-purpose bougainvillea green
there's a sense that everyone's gone to the moon
as in the old song, and you may be imagining
the stillness, but no, everything's poised,
on its mark, holding its collective breath
your skull feels the size of a beach-ball, similarly
weightless, any moment you'll slip your moorings
float up into the welcoming branches of this
blue-gum, join the silent throng of swallows

Cath Kenneally is the author of four collections of poetry, the second of which, *Around Here*, won the John Bray National Poetry Award in 2002. Her latest collection is *Ci Vediamo* (2005). She has just completed a PhD in Creative Writing at Adelaide University.

NEW FROM GIRAMONDO PUBLISHING
THREE COLLECTIONS OF ESSAYS

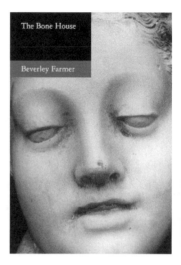

Gerald Murnane
Invisible Yet Enduring Lilacs

An introduction to the curious and eccentric imagination of Gerald Murnane, author of *The Plains*, and one of the masters of contemporary Australian fiction. Essays on Melbourne in the 1950s, Marcel Proust and Jack Kerouac, racehorses and grasslands and learning Hungarian late in life.
$24.95

Louis Nowra
Chihuahuas, Women and Me

The wide range of Nowra's interests is evident in these provocative and compelling essays, on subjects from writing for theatre and film, to Chateaubriand and chihuahuas, porn stars and screen goddesses, the sex appeal of refugees and the Russian new rich.
$27.95

Beverley Farmer
The Bone House

An extended meditation on the life of the body and the life of the mind from one of our most highly respected writers, in three long essays composed of myth, poetry and fable, and personal observation, and woven around the elemental symbols of earth and water, fire and blood, light and darkness.
$29.95

Giramondo books are available from all good bookshops.
As a special offer, we are pleased to send you all three books for the combined price of $66 (including GST and postage), a saving of 20% on RRP.
Please post or email your details to us with cheque or credit card payment.

Giramondo Publishing Company, PO Box 752, Artarmon NSW 1570 AUSTRALIA
books@giramondopublishing.com   www.giramondopublishing.com   tel/fax (02) 9419 7934